FOR REFERENCE

Do Not Take From This Room

POPULAR
MUSIC

The Popular Music Series

Popular Music, 1980–1989, is a revised cumulation of and supersedes Volumes 9 through 14 of the *Popular Music* series, all of which are still available:

Volume 9, 1980–84   Volume 10, 1985
Volume 11, 1986   Volume 12, 1987
Volume 13, 1988   Volume 14, 1989

Popular Music, 1920–1979, is also a revised cumulation of and supersedes Volumes 1 through 8 of the *Popular Music* series, of which Volumes 6 through 8 are still available:

Volume 1, 2nd ed., 1950–59   Volume 2, 1940–49
Volume 3, 1960–64   Volume 4, 1930–39
Volume 5, 1920–29   Volume 6, 1965–69
Volume 7, 1970–74   Volume 8, 1975–79

Popular Music, 1900–1919, is a companion volume to the revised cumulation.

This series continues with:

Volume 15, 1990   Volume 16, 1991
Volume 17, 1992   Volume 18, 1993
Volume 19, 1994   Volume 20, 1995
Volume 21, 1996   Volume 22, 1997
Volume 23, 1998   Volume 24, 1999
Volume 25, 2000

Other Books by Gary Graff

MusicHound Country: The Essential Album Guide

MusicHound Folk: The Essential Album Guide

MusicHound Jazz: The Essential Album Guide

MusicHound Lounge: The Essential Album Guide

MusicHound R&B: The Essential Album Guide

MusicHound Rock: The Essential Album Guide

ISSN 0886-442X

VOLUME 26
2001

POPULAR MUSIC

An Annotated Guide to American Popular Songs,
Including Introductory Essay, Lyricists & Composers Index,
Important Performances Index,
Awards Index, and List of Publishers

GARY GRAFF
Editor

ANDREW C. CLAPS
Project Editor

GALE®

THOMSON

GALE

Detroit • New York • San Diego • San Francisco • Cleveland
New Haven, Conn. • Waterville, Maine • London • Munich

Popular Music, Volume 26

Gary Graff

Project Editor
Andrew C. Claps

Editorial
Michael T. Reade

Composition and Electronic Prepress
Evi Seoud

Manufacturing
Stacy Melson

Product Design
Michael Logusz

Editorial Systems Support
Charles Beaumont, Venus Little

LIBRARY OF CONGRESS CATALOG CARD NUMBER 85-653754

ISBN 0-7876-3313-5
ISSN 0886-442X

Printed in the United States of America
10 9 8 7 6 5 4 3 2 1

Contents

About the Book and How to Use It

This volume is the twenty-sixth in a series whose aim is to set down in permanent and practical form a selective, annotated list of the significant popular songs of our times. Other indexes of popular music have either dealt with special areas, such as jazz or theater and film music, or been concerned chiefly with songs that achieved a degree of popularity as measured by the music-business trade indicators, which vary widely in reliability.

Annual Publication Schedule

The first nine volumes in the *Popular Music* series covered sixty-five years of song history in increments of five or ten years. With Volume 10, a new, annual publication schedule was initiated, making background information available as soon as possible after a song achieves prominence. Yearly publication also allows deeper coverage—approximately five hundred songs—with additional details about writers' inspirations, uses of songs, album appearances, and more.

Indexes Provide Additional Access

Three indexes make the valuable information in the song listings even more accessible to users. The Lyricists & Composers Index shows all the songs represented in *Popular Music, Volume 26,* that are credited to a given individual. The Important Performances Index tells at a glance which albums, musicals, films, television shows, or other media are represented in the volume. The "Performer" category—first added to the index as "Vocalist" in Volume 11—allows the user to see which songs an artist has been associated with this year. The index is arranged by broad media category, then alphabetically by show or album title, with the songs listed under each title. Finally, the Awards Index provides a list of songs nominated for awards by the American Academy of Motion Picture Arts and Sciences (Academy Award) and the American Academy of

Recording Arts and Sciences (Grammy Award). Winning songs are indicated by asterisks.

List of Publishers

The List of Publishers is an alphabetically arranged directory that provides addresses—when available—for the publishers of songs represented in *Popular Music, Volume 26*. Also noted is the organization that handles performance rights for the particular publisher: in the United States, the American Society of Composers, Authors, and Publishers (ASCAP) or Broadcast Music, Inc. (BMI); in Canada, the Society of Composers, Authors, and Music Publishers of Canada (SOCAN); and in Europe, the Society of European Songwriters and Composers (SESAC).

Tracking Down Information on Songs

Unfortunately, the basic records kept by the active participants in the music business are often casual, inaccurate, and transitory. There is no single source of comprehensive information about popular songs, and those sources that do exist do not offer complete information about even the musical works with which they are directly concerned. Four of the primary proprietors of basic information about popular music are the major performing-rights societies: ASCAP, BMI, SOCAN, and SESAC. Although these organizations have considerable information about the songs of their own writer and publisher members, their electronic files are designed primarily for clearance identification by commercial users of music. The files, while extensive in scope, are not necessarily exhaustive, and the facts given about the songs are also limited. ASCAP, BMI, SOCAN, and SESAC are, however, invaluable and indispensable sources of data about popular music.

Another basic source of information about musical compositions and their creators and publishers is the Copyright Office of the Library of Congress. A computerized file lists each published, unpublished, republished, and renewed copyright of songs registered with the Office. There is a time lag (typically a number of months) from the time of application until songs are officially registered (in some cases, songs have already been released before copyright registration begins). This file is helpful in determining the precise date of the declaration of original ownership of musical works, but since some authors, composers, and publishers have been known to employ rather makeshift methods of protecting their works legally, there are songs listed in *Popular Music* that might not be found in the Library of Congress files.

Selection Criteria

In preparing the original volumes for this time period, the staff was faced with a number of separate problems. The first and most important of these was that of selection. The stated aim of the project—to offer the user as comprehensive and accurate a listing of significant popular songs as possible—has been the guiding criterion. The purpose has never been to offer a judgment on the quality of any songs or to indulge a prejudice for or against any type of popular music. Rather, it is the purpose of *Popular Music* to document those musical works that (a) achieved a substantial degree of popular acceptance, (b) were exposed to the public in especially notable circumstances, or (c) were accepted and given important performances by influential musical and dramatic artists.

Another problem was whether or not to classify the songs as to type. Most works of music are subject to any number of interpretations, and although it is possible to describe a particular performance, it is more difficult to give a musical composition a label applicable not only to its origin but also to its subsequent musical history. In fact, the most significant versions of some songs are often quite at variance with the songs' origins. Citations for such songs in *Popular Music* indicate the important facts about not only the songs' origins but also their subsequent lives, rather than assigning an arbitrary and possibly misleading label.

Research Sources

The principal sources of information for the titles, authors, composers, publishers, and dates of copyright of the songs in this volume were ASCAP, BMI, SOCAN, SESAC, the Copyright Office of the Library of Congress, and album notes. For historical notes; information about foreign, folk, public domain, and classical origins; and identification of theatrical, film, and television introducers of songs, the staff relied upon *Billboard* magazine, album notes, Web sites such as All Music Guide (http://www.allmusic.com), CDNOW (http://www.cdnow.com), and Rock on the Net (http://www.rockonthenet.com), and other materials.

Contents of a Typical Entry

The primary listing for a song includes

- title
- author(s) and composer(s)
- current publishers, copyright date
- annotation on the song's origins or performance history

About the Book and How to Use It

Title. The full title—and, when appropriate, alternate title—is given as it appears in the preponderance of the source material. Since even a casual perusal of the book reveals considerable variation in spelling and punctuation, it should be noted that these are the colloquialisms of the music trade and that every effort has been made to capture the most reliable and accurate data possible.

Authorship. In all cases, the primary listing reports the author(s) and composer(s). The reader may find variations in the spelling of a songwriter's name. This results from the fact that some writers used different forms of their names at different times or in connection with different songs. In addition to this kind of variation in the spelling of writers' names, the reader will also notice that in some cases, where the writer is also the performer, the name as writer may differ from the form of the name used as performer.

Publisher. The current publisher or publishers are listed. Since *Popular Music* is designed as a practical reference work rather than an academic study, and since copyrights more than occasionally change hands, the current publisher is given instead of the original copyright holder.

Annotation. The primary listing mentions significant details about the song's history, including performer; album, film, or other production in which the song was introduced or featured; any other performers appearing on the song; record company; awards; and other relevant data. The name of a performer may be listed differently in connection with different songs, especially over a period of years. The name listed is the form of the name given in connection with a particular performance or record. Dates are provided for important recordings and performances.

Popular Music in 2001

For the first eight months of 2001, the tides of the music industry ebbed and flowed like clockwork, with a rather ordinary sampling of music business stories jockeying for position as the year's most important and defining events.

The Beatles' *1,* a hits collection whose youngest song was thirty-one years old, was raising eyebrows—and profit reports—on its way to becoming the No. 1 album on *Billboard*'s year-end chart. Meanwhile, rap-rockers Linkin Park were logging the year's best-selling set of new material, beating out formidable pop competition such as *NSYNC, Shaggy, and Destiny's Child.

Teen pop, so dominant during the previous few years, seemed to be on the wane, while rock—the basic, meat 'n' potatoes, guitar-driven variety—surged back into favor, thanks to bands such as Nickelback, Creed, Staind, Lifehouse, Train, and U2, who captivated the world with passionate, inventive concert performances in support of its Grammy-winning album *All That You Can't Leave Behind.* Hip-hop remained strong but, in lieu of no new releases from genre leaders such as Eminem, Dr. Dre, and Nelly, seemed in search of a real focal point.

Young R&B diva Alicia Keys was the consensus best new arrival of the year—both critically and commercially—though the versatile, genre-splicing Canadian singer Nelly Furtado floated like a butterfly and sang like a bird. And the roots music soundtrack to the film *O Brother, Where Art Thou?* staged a quiet but plucky revolution that brought American mountain music into the pop culture mainstream, though no one was betting heavily on a permanent turn of tastes in that direction. The continuing battle against Napster and the general subject of on-line downloading, both authorized and bootlegged, were consuming issues throughout the year.

All told, it was business as usual. Until the second Monday in September.

Darkness on the Edge of Town

As they did to every other sector of society, the September 11 terrorist attacks on New York City and Washington, D.C., eclipsed all other matters in the music industry. The short-term impact brought operations to a temporary standstill: Tours were halted, promotions were postponed, and some album releases were rescheduled. Groups such as Train, Incubus, and the Cranberries reedited videos to eliminate troubling, violent images. The British band Bush changed the cover of its album *Golden State* to remove the image of an airplane, and changed the title of its single from "Speed Kills" to "The People That We Love."

Modern progressive-rockers Dream Theater had to change the cover of its live album *Live Scenes From New York,* which depicted the World Trade Center and the Statue of Liberty aflame, while hip-hop act the Coup, whose *Party Music* was considered one of the year's best rap albums, altered its cover art, which featured group leader Raymond "Boots" Riley triggering an explosion at the Trade Center towers. Meanwhile, New York's own Strokes, one of the hottest bands of the so-called new garage scene, was successfully pressured by its label, RCA Records, to remove the pejorative track "New York City Cops" from the domestic version of its debut album, *Is This It.*

Musicians quickly threw their energies into helping raise funds for relief efforts. Just ten days after the tragedies, on September 21, artists such as Bruce Springsteen, Billy Joel, U2, Celine Dion, Alicia Keys, Limp Bizkit, and others gathered in New York and Los Angeles for the "America: A Tribute to Heroes" telethon, which raised an estimated $150 million. In October, ex-Beatle Paul McCartney—who witnessed the attacks from the Kennedy Airport tarmac—spearheaded the all-star Concert for New York, at which he debuted "Freedom," a song he hastily added to his *Driving Rain* album. Aerosmith, the Backstreet Boys (who lost a staff member in one of the flights that crashed into the Trade Center towers), Destiny's Child, and others staged a similar concert in Washington, D.C., while Peter Frampton led a cadre of classic-rockers in Cincinnati.

Other responses were a bit more reactionary. The Clear Channel radio chain issued a lengthy list of songs it recommended its stations not play, including acclaimed and benign selections such as John Lennon's "Imagine" and Simon and Garfunkel's "Bridge Over Troubled Water." "I thought that was the most ridiculous damn list I'd ever heard," said Neil Young, who performed "Imagine" during the "America: A Tribute to Heroes" telethon. "That just illustrates completely how out of touch with reality some of these people can get, the programmers and all these people, deciding what's cool to play and what isn't cool to play. We don't need advice on what we should listen to and what we should play. I thought it was a joke, really. 'Bridge Over Troubled Water'; what the hell's wrong with *that* song?"

Young was one of the first musicians to respond in song to the September 11 attacks. Finishing work on his 2002 album *Are You Passionate?*, he wrote a song called "Let's Roll," which took its title from words spoken by United Airlines Flight 93 passenger Todd Beamer before he and his fellow passengers attacked their hijackers and brought down the plane— thought to be headed toward a target in Washington, D.C.—in a western Pennsylvania field.

"Let's Roll" is at once a chronicle and a tribute to those who, according to Young, felt "You got to turn on evil when it's coming after you." "There was no effort made to make it actually factual; it's just basically an image of what happened, the way it hit me," Young explained. "It struck me as heroic in a legendary way. It's such a pure example of heroism. There was no reward involved. These guys weren't doing this to be martyrs or because they thought they would get a payback. . . . They just did the right thing. It was so heroic it just had to be captured."

Though country star Alan Jackson's "Where Were You (When the World Stopped Turning)" wasn't released until early 2002, it had its impact on November 7, 2001, when he debuted it at the Country Music Association Awards ceremony and brought the house down, causing radio programmers to begin airing the performance from the show, and his record company, Arista, to rush-release the studio version to stations. Georgia Congressman Mac Collins even had the lyrics read into the *Congressional Record* upon their release.

The song, Jackson said, came to him one night in late October, though the concept had been gestating for quite some time. "Ever since [the attacks] happened, everybody I know who writes songs had a lot of emotion they wanted to put to music," explained the former Ford truck pitchman. "I had ideas, but they just didn't feel right. Then this song came out, like a gift from God, really. I put it on tape that night, got up the next morning and finished it, and it's just been flying ever since."

There were other "songs of healing" that clearly comforted audiences during the fall of 2001—among them the Enrique Iglesias crooner "Hero," Five For Fighting's plaintive "Superman (It's Not Easy)," Enya's airy "Only Time," Nickelback's charged "How You Remind Me," and Creed's anthemic "My Sacrifice." Creed front man Scott Stapp, in fact, felt that the band's entire third album, *Weathered,* was filled with songs that could have been inspired by the events of September 11, even if, like the others, they were conceived and recorded well before then.

"I definitely think that people are gonna perceive some of these songs a lot differently because of that," he said. "Some of [the songs] may even seem like they were written because of that. Every single one of these songs was written in March. . . . We attribute it to just being in tune with the world and our personal struggles when we translate them into songs."

By and large, however, songwriters and musicians struggled with their role in the wake of September 11. "I had to think, 'What the hell am I gonna say here that's gonna matter?'" noted Robert Flynn of the heavy metal band Machine Head. "I understand what we are in the big picture of things. We make music. We're an escape. If anything, what we can try to do is give people a soundtrack to live their life, to pull them through the good times and help them through the bad times."

Even at the "America: A Tribute to Heroes" telethon, Billy Joel said he felt "kind of irrelevant. I'm glad I could do something; it wasn't nearly enough. Something like this makes you feel very inadequate, really. We were meeting and greeting backstage, giving each other kinda chagrined shrugs like, 'Well, at least we can try to do something.'"

Rockin' in the Free World

The all-encompassing impact made by September 11 aside, musicians did, in reality, do plenty of things throughout the rest of 2001. One of the most interesting trends was dubbed the "return of rock"—a veritable cavalcade of hits built on elements such as crunch, volume, and muscle, all of which had been plowed under by the teen-pop phenomenon of the late '90s and early 2000s.

Creed was no stranger to this trend; the Florida outfit, which debuted in 1997, helped to set it in motion with its multiplatinum first two albums. *Weathered* was sure to be a hit, too, but *how* big a hit was the question. The answer: a very big hit. Though released just six weeks before the end of the year, *Weathered* debuted at No. 1 in its first week of sale and moved a whopping 3.5 million copies, becoming the eighth-highest seller of the year.

"We did everything the same way we did on the first two albums; we just wrote until we felt like we had a record and made an album," explained Scott Stapp. However, Stapp did credit the success of the first two albums with giving Creed "an opportunity, financially to spend more money on this record and offer a little bit more ear candy for the fans." That included Cherokee chanter Bo Taylor for the song "Who's Got My Back?" and the Tallahassee Boys' Choir on "Don't Stop Dancing," a track that also featured Stapp's younger sister Amie on vocals.

"The success afforded us the opportunity to have more resources and to experiment a little more with the concepts in our heads," Stapp said.

"And it wasn't that we felt like we couldn't do it on the first two; it was just 'cause, financially, we couldn't do it."

If Creed stoked mass appetites for rock with its earlier albums, 2001 was the year other bands offered up a feast. Nickelback blew the roof off with its hit "How You Remind Me." Puddle of Mudd, discovered by Limp Bizkit front man Fred Durst, won fans with "Control" and other songs from its debut album, *Come Clean*. Staind scored with "Fade" and "It's Been Awhile," while Fuel delivered a "Hemorrhage (In My Hands)."

Weezer returned from a six-year absence with a self-titled third album and hits such as "Hash Pipe" and "Island in the Sun." The power ballad also remained a hot rock commodity, with the likes of Eve 6's "Here's to the Night" and "Be Like That" from 3 Doors Down—who continued the momentum of its 2000 hit, "Kryptonite," with tracks such as "Duck and Run" and "Loser." Even the Cult, an '80s and '90s hero of the hard- and alternative-rock markets, regrouped to release its first album in seven years, while Ozzy Osbourne's *Down to Earth* brought the Black Sabbath bad boy back to the solo route for the first time in seven years.

"It's a good time to be a rock band again," noted Nickelback's Chad Kroeger. "I think a lot of the little kids who got turned on to music by Britney [Spears] or the Backstreet Boys, now they're wanting something maybe a little bit different or a little more dangerous-sounding, so they turn to rock."

Rock's own trendier subgenres thrived as well. Blink-182 ("The Rock Show") and Green Day ("Warning") continued to lead the nuevo punk posse, which welcomed new heroes such as Sum 41 ("Fat Lip") and Alien Ant Farm, whose remake of "Smooth Criminal" gave Michael Jackson his greatest burst of popularity since his moonwalking glory days of the '80s.

Rap-rock remained paced by Limp Bizkit, which maintained the success of its 2000 album, *Chocolate St*rfish and the Hot Dog Flavored Water*, with tracks such as "My Way." But the kings of that form were also the kings of the cash registers: Linkin Park charged out of Los Angeles to sell more than 4.8 million copies of its debut album, *Hybrid Theory*, making it the No. 1 seller of 2001. It also answered skeptics who wondered whether fans would really embrace another band meshing strident raps with metallic guitars.

"We started basically just with a stylistic idea of wanting to meld our love of hip-hop and that style of music with our love of really heavy kind of alternative rock stuff," explained guitarist Brad Delson. "That was before the whole wave of rap-rock bands kind of surfaced.

"Without making comparisons, I'd say our music is definitely very emotional. It's very introspective. It's not the tough, 'We're gonna kick your ass' kind of music. It's more like 'This is how we feel,' and we want to present it in a really sincere way."

The critics' choice of the rock revival, meanwhile, was System of a Down, the strident Armenian band from Los Angeles whose sophomore album, *Toxicity,* debuted at No. 1 in its first week of release. It was a particularly brutal album, musically and lyrically, but the group wasn't about to apologize for pointed songs such as "Prison Song," "Chop Suey!" or "ATWA," guitarist Daron Malakian's embrace of Charles Manson's environmental views.

"Any good poet, I think, has a good thumb on the heartbeat of the times. I think good music does that as well," said System of a Down front man Serge Tankian. "It doesn't have to be political or social to do so, either; it could be a simple love song, or it could be anything that touches the emotions of the time. That's what we try to create, something that's universal and timeless."

Pop Gets Its Hands Dirty

And what of the music that rock was purportedly beginning to supplant? It was hardly a bad year for pop: Britney Spears' third album, *Britney,* sold 750,000 copies in its first week of release, while *NSYNC's *Celebrity* notched 1.88 million sales during its first week and went on to move more than 4.4 million copies, becoming the top-selling album released in the 2001 calendar year. Even O-Town, the group assembled before a nation of viewers on ABC's *Making the Band,* scored a platinum debut album along with hits such as "Liquid Dreams" and "All or Nothing."

Yet they and mates such as Destiny's Child, the Backstreet Boys, and scores of others were surrounded by whispers and speculation that their style of music was on the wane, with CD sales and concert tickets in decline and a general subsidence of the overall mania that marked previous years. The screams were still there, it seemed, but the decibel levels were declining.

*NSYNC addressed these charges in "Pop," the first single from *Celebrity*: "Sick and tired of hearing all these people talking about / What's the deal with this pop life and when's it gonna be fading out?" "Pop will never die," said the band's Justin Timberlake, who cowrote and coproduced "Pop" and attracted as much attention for his relationship with Spears as he did for his musical pursuits.

"If rock takes over, it's what's gonna become pop, 'cause pop is popular music," said Timberlake. "The style of music we do is so intertwined with rock elements and hip-hop elements and dance beat elements that people don't know how to classify it. But pop music will always be around; if it's not in the shape of us, maybe it's in the shape of Sum 41."

Timberlake's bandmate Lance Bass believed that a backlash against the boys and girls who ruled the charts was inevitable. "I mean, it's been enormous," he said. "I think we're very lucky to be one of the ones that kinda stand out. It's terrible for a new pop group or pop act right now; all the new pop artists are kinda getting lost in the dust. Nobody really cares anymore. . . .

"So a lot of the baby acts will be disappearing . . . and the ones that really made it and stand up will last. Like in the '80s when pop was huge; it was Madonna and Michael Jackson and Janet Jackson, and look at 'em now. They continue to do what they do even though they've been through phases when pop wasn't big. They already established themselves and they had their fan base and they were always huge."

More and more in 2001, it seemed like survival in pop required media diversification—cheerfully lampooned in the film version of *Josie and the Pussycats.* Even as *Britney* came out, Spears was hyping her 2002 film debut, *Crossroads,* while Bass coproduced and starred in *On the Line,* with fellow *NSYNCer Joey Fatone in a supporting role. O-Town had the TV hook, as did Eden's Crush, a female counterpart formed by a similar TV-based talent search. Another all-female group, Dream, had the benefit of label chief and executive producer Sean "P. Diddy" Combs' fashion and entertainment empire.

Maturity also became an issue for the whole pop movement—illustrated no more clearly than in Spears' album, in which she mined more overtly sexual themes and lamented the difficulties of being "a girl, not yet a woman."

"I'm verging on being a woman," she explained, "which is kind of hard. Since I've grown up in the spotlight, people place these things on you in a certain way—not necessarily my fans or anything, but people around me. They treat you a certain way when you're 16 or 17, and it's up to you to stand up and say 'I need my own identity and need to do those things on my own.' I think a lot of teenagers can relate to that.

"And I think when you grow as a person, you're gonna grow as an artist as well. I just think for this, my third album, I had to grow creatively. I couldn't do . . . *Baby One More Time* number three. I just had to change it up a little bit and just pray people would think that's cool, or appreciate it or really love my music."

Destiny Calls

It was another solid year for the R&B/pop trio Destiny's Child. Its third album, *Survivor,* sold more than 3.7 million copies and launched hits such as "Bootylicious," a smooth cover of Samantha Sang's Bee Gees–written hit "Emotion," and the title track. Save for the minor miscue of sporting some Los Angeles Lakers jerseys during a halftime show at an NBA championship game in Philadelphia, the group was in fine form all year. It even accomplished the rare task of entering some new terminology into the pop culture lexicon: "bootylicious" and that song's reference to "jelly."

"Jelly is like your mojo, whatever you have that makes you feel confident," explained group leader Beyonce Knowles, who was signed to costar in the third installment of the mojo-istic *Austin Powers* movie series. "It can be your butt. It can be your hair, your eyes, your mind, your attitude, whatever. It's whatever makes you feel good."

Knowles initially felt that the whole song was "too dumb" to even present to her bandmates, but they convinced her otherwise. "I walked into Gadzooks and I saw a 'Bootylicious' T-shirt. And every magazine I pick up, they have a column that's 'Bootylicious,' and it's just like, 'Whoa, that's weird. This is strange.' But I'm glad it took."

Destiny's Child approached the end of 2001 with some daring plans. Following a Christmas album, each of the group's members planned to record a solo album, starting with a gospel effort from Michelle Williams. In addition, Knowles' younger sister Solange, who performed the title song for the Disney Channel cartoon *The Proud Family,* was planning her own solo debut.

But Knowles said there's no question that destiny will bring her, Williams, and Kelly Rowland back together, probably sooner rather than later.

"We need a break," Knowles said. "But Destiny's Child is the three of us. You can't get that feeling by yourself that we feel when the three of us are together, the harmony, the chemistry, all of that. Destiny's Child is blissfully happy right now, and there's something about a group, when you truly love it and your voices sound so good together—you know you can't give that up for anything."

Don't Stop 'Til You Get Enough

By most measures, it was a good year for the Jackson family. But Michael and Janet, accustomed to multiplatinum success on a mega scale, found it bitterly disappointing.

Though his comeback was ballyhooed with everything from an all-star TV special/concert to a surprise performance with *NSYNC on the MTV Video Music Awards, Michael Jackson's first album in more than six years was hardly *Invincible* and showed that the self-proclaimed King of Pop had little luster left on his crown. The album did debut at No. 1 in the U.S. in November—with first-week sales of 366,272 copies—and in twelve other countries, but was replaced the following week by Britney Spears' *Britney* and was never able to make a lasting impact on the album or singles charts. And an all-star recording he planned as a benefit for September 11 victims was still missing in action well into 2002.

Janet Jackson, meanwhile, had a slightly better go of it. Her *All For You* debuted at No. 1 in the spring, selling 605,000 copies in its first week, though it was knocked out of the top spot by Destiny's Child just seven days later. Still, she enjoyed continued success throughout the year, thanks to a lavish tour and hits such as "Someone to Call My Lover" and the title track.

Even as *All For You* was released, however, Jackson acknowledged that her title as pop's reigning diva had been usurped by younger performers, including some who even copped a few of her own trademarks.

"I hear it with Britney when she says 'Stop!' or 'Sing!'; that definitely reminded me of myself," Jackson said. "But mostly I just see them as other dance artists like myself, people who love to dance and perform.

"It's flattering, though; it doesn't anger me. I always try to stay true to myself and write what I'm feeling, what goes on in my life and what moves me. I don't feel that I have to go out or go above and beyond them. I am very competitive, but, no, not like that."

A Shaggy Dawg Story

On his hit "Angel," the reggae-pop star Shaggy rapped, "I wanna show the nation my appreciation." And well he should.

Popular Music in 2001

Shaggy's *Hotshot,* released in 2000, was 2001's second-best seller, with more than 4.5 million copies sold. Few successes were this sweet; he had been booted off his previous label, and even his current company, MCA, didn't agree with him that the album's first two smash hits, "It Wasn't Me" and "Angel," should be released as singles.

"I spotted ['It Wasn't Me' and 'Angel'] as singles from day one," recalls the Jamaican-born reggae toaster, now a resident of Brooklyn, New York. "But I had just changed labels, from Virgin to MCA, and I got to MCA on the strength of a hit, 'Luv Me Luv Me,' which was produced by [Jimmy] Jam and [Terry] Lewis. So they went with another Jam and Lewis release ['Dance and Shout']; that was the real chemistry, to them. But what's happened since has pretty much shown that the chemistry really lies with my own production team, which did 'Angel' and 'It Wasn't Me.'"

"It Wasn't Me" introduced the phrase "bangin' on the bathroom floor" into the adolescent lexicon, much to the consternation of parents everywhere. But Shaggy says any concern about that was mitigated by the fact that the song actually castigates men who sneak around and cheat on their women.

"I talk about relationships for the simple fact I think everyone can relate," he said. "I talk about some shit and make fun about it and hit some true points that other people would not hit on their records. I sit down and think about situations that are interesting, like a writer would write a fiction story. I look for subject matter that's gonna grab people and say 'Hey, let's hit this.'"

"Falling" for the First Time

The entertainment world suffered a substantial loss when singer and actress Aaliyah perished in an August 25 plane crash in the Bahamas. But 2001 saw the rise of two newcomers who, if they didn't entirely fill the void, certainly became strong presences at the pop and R&B crossroads that Aaliyah once ruled.

Alicia Keys was, without question, the best new arrival of the year, selling more than 4.1 million copies of her debut album, *Songs in A Minor,* driven by the sultry, smoky hit "Falling." One part piano-playing soul classicist and one part modernist, the New York artist was among those executive Clive Davis took with him to his new J Records label when he was ousted from Arista. Along with O-Town, Keys helped Davis establish the fresh imprint as a force in the music industry.

But if Keys seemed a bit, well, serious, Canada's Nelly Furtado was her spirited foil, a genre-blending alchemist of Portuguese descent who could be pretty and earnest on "I'm Like a Bird" and then playful and street-smart on "Turn Off the Light" and "Shit on the Radio (Remember the Days)." Before the year was out, Furtado found herself collaborating with Mary J. Blige and trading grooves with Moby and others on the inaugural Area:One tour.

"I find the pop thing really fun now," Furtado said. "Pop gives me this great freedom. You still get to see kind of a cross-section of what's going on in music. It's fun that I can be the vanguard of all these other styles within the pop world; it makes me stand out from my peers.

"That's why I make pop music. It's a challenge to create songs that have integrity but connects with the collective unconscious. I love that challenge; I love the idea of tapping into something on such a large scale. It's a science."

Down From the Mountain

Amid the glitzier battles over pop trends, a quiet and entirely unexpected revolution took place in the marketplace. Listeners—particularly adults looking for a sound of their own to embrace among the hip-hop, rap-rock, and teen pop favored by their children—were entranced by the homespun soundtrack to the Coen brothers' late-2000 film, *O Brother, Where Art Thou?*

A serious, scholarly helping of bluegrass, country, folk, and other American roots musics of the Depression era, the *O Brother* soundtrack didn't exactly have the Britneys of the world quaking in their designer boots. But then something totally unexpected happened. Despite limited airplay, the album became a phenomenon, selling nearly 3.5 million copies and spinning off an unexpected hit in "I Am a Man of Constant Sorrow" by the fictional Soggy Bottom Boys (composed of Alison Krauss & Union Station multi-instrumentalist Dan Tyminski, Harley Allen, and Pat Enright). It also inspired a concert tour that became the subject of D. A. Pennebaker's documentary *Down From the Mountain*.

It was the banjo pluck—or the mandolin strum—heard 'round the world, and it had makers of bluegrass and other styles represented in the film open-mouthed with shock. And pleasure.

"I never imagined it would be such a big deal—going in, I don't think anybody did," said Tyminski. "I'm still scratching my head trying to figure out what happened."

T-Bone Burnett, the singer-songwriter who compiled the soundtrack—and subsequently launched a new label, DMZ Records, with the Coen brothers—simply adhered to the theory that if you present an audience with good music and rich talent (ranging from old-timers such as Ralph Stanley and the Fairfield Four to the more contemporary likes of Emmylou Harris and Gillian Welch), they will come.

"I think it has its place in the culture or something, different levels of people trying to hold onto or not lose who we are," Burnett said. "There was a lot of good energy brought to bear around this whole thing, and a tremendous amount of talent was brought to bear on it. A lot of incredibly gifted people came to the show. It was a good happenstance, you know? It was a good thing that went down, and people dug it—which is even better."

No one came out of the *O Brother* experience predicting that bluegrass or other roots musics could ultimately take over the world. But for a wonderfully pure moment, they did just that, bringing some much-needed light to a dark, troubling year.

—Gary Graff
Editor

A

Absolutely Not
Words and music by James Glasco, Darrin Jennings, Eric Johnson, Eric
  Jones, Tiffany Palmer, and Ahmad Russell
TCF Music Publishing, 2001/Glasco Music, Co., 2001/Axis Media
  Publishing, 2001/Aruss Music, 2001/Deondre's Bird, 2001/EMI-April
  Music, 2001
Performed by Deborah Cox on the movie soundtrack album *Dr. Dolittle
  2* (J Records, 2001).

After Party
Words and music by Nathan Butler, Teron Beal, Joel Campbell, Star
  Gordon, Willieque Gilchrist, and Eritza Laues
Al's Street Music, 2000/BMG Songs Inc., 2000/Faith Force, 2000/Teron
  Beal Songs, 2000/WB Music Publishing, 2000/Zomba Enterprises,
  2000/Magic Man Music, 2000
Performed by Koffee Brown on the album *Mars/Venus* (Arista, 2001).

Ain't Nobody Here but Us Chickens
Words and music by Alex Kramer and Joan Whitney
The Bourne Co., 1947
Covered by Asleep at the Wheel on the album *The Very Best of Asleep
  at the Wheel* (Relentless, 2001). Originally performed by Louis
  Jordan. Nominated for a Grammy Award, Best Country Performance
  by a Duo/Group With Vocal, 2001.

Ain't Nothing 'Bout You
Words and music by Melvern Rutherford, II and Tom Shapiro
Memphisto Music, 2001/Universal-MCA Music Publishing, 2001/Tree
  Publishing, 2001/Wenonga Music, 2001
Performed by Brooks and Dunn on the album *Steers & Stripes* (Arista
  Nashville, 2001). Nominated for a Grammy Award, Best Country
  Performance by a Duo/Group With Vocal, 2001.

Alive
Words and music by Noah Bernado, Marcos Curiel, Mark Daniels, and

Paul Sandoval
Famous Music Corp., 2001/Souljah Music, 2001
Performed by P.O.D. on the album *Satellite* (Atlantic, 2001). Nominated for a Grammy Award, Best Hard Rock Performance, 2001.

All Night Long
Words and music by Bruce Brown, Charles Daniels, William DiGregorio, John Gavin, and Charles Hayward
Miss Hazel Music, 1993/Songs of Universal, 1993
Covered by Montgomery Gentry featuring Charlie Daniels on the album *Tattoos & Scars* (Columbia, 1999). Originally performed by Charlie Daniels on the album *America, I Believe in You* (Liberty, 1993).

All or Nothing
Words and music by Wayne Hector and Steve Mac (pseudonym for Steve McCutcheon)
Irving Music Inc., 2001/Songs of Windswept Pacific, 2001/Rokstone Music, 2001/Universal-MCA Music Publishing, 2001
Performed by O-Town on the album *O-Town* (J Records, 2001).

All the Way to Reno (You're Gonna Be a Star)
Words and music by Peter Buck, Michael Mills, and Michael Stipe
Temporary Music, 2001
Performed by R.E.M. on the album *Reveal* (Warner Bros., 2001).

All for You
Words and music by Janet Jackson, Terry Lewis, and James Harris, III, music by Wayne Garfield, Mauro Malavasi, and David Romani
Arapesh Communications, 2000/Flyte Tyme Tunes, 2000/Little Macho Music, 2000/Black Ice Publishing, 2000
Performed by Janet Jackson on the album *All for You* (Virgin, 2001). Won a Grammy Award for Best Dance Recording, 2001.

Alright
Words and music by Jeff Lynne
EMI-April Music, 2001
Performed by the Electric Light Orchestra on the album *Zoom* (Epic, 2001).

Always With Me, Always With You
Music by Joe Satriani
Strange Beautiful Music, 1987
Performed by Joe Satriani on the album *Live in San Francisco* (Epic, 2001). Originally featured on the album *Surfing With the Alien* (Relativity, 1987). Nominated for a Grammy Award, Best Rock Instrumental Performance, 2001.

AM to PM
Words and music by Christian Karlsson, Manuel Lopez, Christina

Milian, and Pontus Winnberg
Deston Songs, 2001/Havana Brown Publishing, 2001/Murlyn Songs, 2001/Songs of Universal, 2001
Performed by Christina Milian on the album *Christina Milian* (Island/Def Jam, 2001).

Androgyny
Words and music by Douglas Erickson, Shirley Manson, Steve Marker, and Butch Vig
Almo Music Corp., 2001/Deadarm Music, 2001/Irving Music Inc., 2001/Vibe Crusher Music, 2001
Performed by Garbage on the album *Beautiful Garbage* (Interscope, 2001).

Angel
Words and music by Paul Barry, Lionel Richie, and Mark Taylor
LBR Music, 2000/Right Bank Music, 2000
Performed by Lionel Richie on the album *Renaissance* (Island, 2001).
Nominated for a Grammy Award, Best Dance Recording, 2001.

Angel
Words and music by Eddie Curtis, Ahmet Ertegun, Steve Miller, and Chip Taylor (pseudonym for James Voight)
Jim Rooster Music, 1967/Sailor Music, 1967/Cotillion Music Inc., 1967/EMI-Blackwood Music Inc., 1967
Performed by Shaggy on the album *Hotshot* (MCA, 2000). Based on the 1968 Merrilee Rush hit "Angel of the Morning."

Angels in Waiting
Words and music by Tammy Cochran, Stewart Harris, and Jim McBride
Peermusic III LTD, 2000/Wide Ocean Music, 2000/Cal IV Entertainment Inc., 2000/O'Shaughnessy Ave Music, 2000/WB Music Publishing, 2000
Performed by Tammy Cochran on the album *Tammy Cochran* (Epic, 2001).

Angry All the Time
Words and music by Bruce Robison
Bruce Robison Music, 1995/Mighty Nice Music, 1995/Tiltawhirl Music, 1995
Covered by Tim McGraw on the album *Set This Circus Down* (Curb, 2001). Originally performed by Bruce Robison on the album *Bruce Robison* (Vireo, 1996).

Answer the Phone
Words and music by Mark McGrath, Rodney Sheppard, Craig Bullock, Charles Frazier, George Gilmore, and Matthew Karges
Four Forty Magnum Music, 2001/Grave Lack of Talent Music, 2001/

Irving Music Inc., 2001/Warner-Tamerlane Publishing, 2001
Performed by Sugar Ray on the album *Sugar Ray* (Lava/Atlantic, 2001).

Answering Bell
Words and music by Ryan Adams
Barland Music, 2001
Performed by Ryan Adams on the album *Gold* (Lost Highway, 2001).

Are You Satisfied?
Words and music by Victor Calderone, Deborah Cooper, and Michael
    Vinciguerra
Little Mike Music, 2001/Vix Mix Music, 2001
Performed by Victor Calderone featuring Deborah Cooper on the album
    E=VC2, Volume 2 (Tommy Boy, 2001).

Area Codes
Words and music by Phalon Alexander, Ludacris (pseudonym for
    Christopher Bridges), Nate Dogg (pseudonym for Nathaniel Hale),
    and William Nichols
EMI-April Music, 2001/Ludacris Music Publishing, 2001/Bill-Lee
    Music, 2001/Bubba Gee Music, 2001/Lehsem Songs, 2001/Music in
    Three, 2001/Nate Dogg Music, 2001/Warner-Tamerlane Publishing,
    2001
Performed by Ludacris featuring Nate Dogg on the movie soundtrack
    album *Rush Hour 2* (Def Jam, 2001). Later featured on the Ludacris
    album *Word of Mouf* (Def Jam, 2001). Nominated for a Grammy
    Award, Best Rap/Sung Collaboration, 2001.

Argument
Words and music by Brendan Canty, Joseph Lally, Ian MacKaye, and
    Guy Picciotto
Fugazi Songs, 2001
Performed by Fugazi on the album *The Argument* (Dischord, 2001).

Ashes by Now
Words and music by Rodney Crowell
Tessa Publishing, 1976
Covered by Lee Ann Womack on the album *I Hope You Dance* (MCA
    Nashville, 2000). Originally performed by Rodney Crowell on the
    album *But What Will the Neighbors Think* (Warner Bros., 1980).

Astounded
Words and music by Dominique Brouillette, Sylvain Brouillette, James
    Di Salvio, and Gary McKenzie, music by Curtis Mayfield
Editorial Avenue, 2001/Warner-Tamerlane Publishing, 2001
Performed by Bran Van 3000 on the album *Discosis* (Virgin, 2001).

Austin
Words and music by David Kent and Kirsti Manna-Warner

Talbot Music Publishing, 2001/Kirsti Mannasongs, 2001
Performed by Blake Shelton on the album *Blake Shelton* (Warner Bros., 2001).

Awake
Words and music by Sully (pseudonym for Salvatore Erna)
Meeengya Music, 2000
Performed by Godsmack on the album *Awake* (Republic/Universal, 2000).

B

Baby If You're Ready
Words and music by Priest Brooks, Chan Gaines, Kevin Gilliam, Kola
   Marion, Kimberley Proby, and LaToya Williams
Black Blessed Girl Music, 2000/Black Fountain Music, 2000/High Priest
   Publishing, 2000/Nay D Publishing, 2000/Show You How Daddy Ball
   Music, 2000/So Kol Productions, 2000/EMI-April Music, 2000
Performed by Doggy's Angels featuring LaToya on the album
   Pleezbaleevit (Doggystyle/TVT, 2000).

Bad Boy for Life
Words and music by Black Rob (pseudonym for Robert Ross), Mark
   Curry, Jamel Fisher, Drayton Goss, and Dorsey Wesley
Diamond Rob Music, 2001/Dors-D Music, 2001/EMI-April Music,
   2001/Justin Combs Publishing, 2001/Bristeasy Music, 2001/EMI-
   Blackwood Music Inc., 2001/Janice Combs Music, 2001/Me Again
   Music, 2001/Dee Mac Music, 2001
Performed by P. Diddy & the Bad Boy Family featuring Black Rob and
   Mark Curry on the album *The Saga Continues* . . . (Bad Boy, 2001).
   Nominated for a Grammy Award, Best Rap Performance by a Duo or
   Group, 2001.

Bad Day
Words and music by Carl Bell
Pener Pig Publishing, 2000/Universal Songs of Polygram Intntl., 2000
Performed by Fuel on the album *Something Like Human* (Epic/550,
   2000).

Ballad of the Boy in the Red Shoes
Words by Bernard Taupin, music by Elton John (pseudonym for
   Reginald Dwight)
Warner-Tamerlane Publishing, 2001/Wretched Music, 2001
Performed by Elton John on the album *Songs From the West Coast*
   (Rocket/Universal, 2001).

The Ballad of Carol Lynn
Words and music by Ryan Adams and Michael Daly
Barland Music, 2001/Caitlin Breanne Music, 2001
Performed by Whiskeytown on the album *Pneumonia* (Lost Highway, 2001).

Basement Apt.
Words and music by Sarah Harmer
Pare Publishing, 2000/Plant Publishing II, 2000
Performed by Sarah Harmer on the album *You Were Here* (Zoe/ Rounder, 2000).

Be Like That
Words and music by Brad Arnold, music by Christopher Henderson
Escatawpa Songs, 2000/Songs of Universal, 2000
Performed by 3 Doors Down on the album *The Better Life* (Republic/ Universal, 2000).

Because I Got High
Words and music by Afroman (pseudonym for Joseph Foreman)
Universal-MCA Music Publishing, 2000
Performed by Afroman on the album *The Good Times* (Universal, 2001). Also featured on the movie soundtrack album *Jay and Silent Bob Strike Back* (Universal, 2001). Nominated for a Grammy Award, Best Rap Solo Performance, 2001.

Beer Run (B Double E Double Are You In?)
Words and music by Keith Anderson, Kent Blazy, George Ducas, Amanda Williams, and Kim Williams
Ducas Music, 2001/EMI-April Music, 2001/Hollohart Music, 2001/ Romeo Cowboy Music, 2001/Sony ATV Tunes LLC, 2001
Performed by George Jones and Garth Brooks on Jones' album *The Rock: Stone Cold Country 2001* (BNA, 2001). Also featured on Brooks' album *Scarecrow* (Capitol Nashville, 2001). Nominated for a Grammy Award, Best Country Collaboration With Vocals, 2001.

Believe in Life
Words and music by Eric Clapton
EC Music Ltd., 2001/Unichappell Music Inc., 2001
Performed by Eric Clapton on the album *Reptile* (Reprise, 2001).

Best I Ever Had (Grey Sky Morning)
Words and music by Matthew Scannell
Mascan Music, 1999/WB Music Publishing, 1999
Performed by Vertical Horizon on the album *Everything You Want* (RCA, 1999).

Best of Things
Words by Xzibit (pseudonym for Alvin Joiner), words and music by Dr.

Dre (pseudonym for Andre Young), music by Michael Elizondo
Ain't Nothing but Funkin', 2000/Blotter Music, 2000/Elvis Mambo
   Music, 2000/Music of Windswept, 2000/WB Music Publishing, 2000/
   Alexra Music, 2000/Hennesy for Everyone, 2000
Performed by Xzibit on the album *Restless* (Relativity, 2000).

Bigacts Littleacts
Words and music by Derrick Harris, Gary Grice, and Afu-Ra
   (pseudonym for Aaron Phillip)
Life Force Music, 2000
Performed by Afu-Ra featuring GZA on the album *Body of the Life
   Force* (Koch, 2000).

Bizounce
Words and music by Joshua Thompson, Douglas Allen, III, David
   Conley, Olivia Longott, Quincy Patrick, and Juan Peters
Dreamworks Songs, 2001/Plaything Music, 2001/Tallest Tree Music,
   2001/Q Zik Music, 2001/Music Pieces, 2001
Performed by Olivia on the album *Olivia* (J Records, 2001).

Bleed American
Words and music by James Adkins, Richard Burch, Zachary Lind, and
   Thomas Linton
Turkey On Rye Music, 2001
Performed by Jimmy Eat World on the album *Bleed American*
   (DreamWorks, 2001).

Blood Pollution
Words and music by Twiggy Ramirez (pseudonym for Jeordie White)
EMI-Blackwood Music Inc., 2001/Bloodheavy Music, 2001/Warner-
   Barham Music LLC, 2001
Performed by the fictional band Steel Dragon on the movie soundtrack
   album *Rock Star* (Priority, 2001).

Blue Moon of Kentucky
Words and music by Bill Monroe
APRS Music, 1947
Covered by Tom Petty & the Heartbreakers on the album *Good Rockin'
   Tonight: The Legacy of Sun Records* (Sire, 2001). Originally
   performed by Bill Monroe.

B.O.B.
Words and music by Antwan Patton, Andre Benjamin, and David Sheats
Chrysalis Music, 2000/Dungeon Rat Music, 2000/EMI-April Music,
   2000/Gnat Booty Music, 2000
Performed by Outkast on the album *Stankonia* (LaFace/Arista, 2000).

Bodies
Words and music by Stephen Benton, Michael Luce, Christian Pierce,

and David Williams
Pounding Drool, 2001/Renfield Music Publishing, 2001
Performed by Drowning Pool on the album *Sinner* (Wind-Up, 2001).

Bootylicious
Words and music by Robert Fusari, Beyonce Knowles, and Falonte
  Moore, music by Stevie Nicks
Welsh Witch Music, 2001/Obo Itself, 2001/Beyonce Publishing, 2001/
  June Bug Alley, 2001/Lonte Music, 2001/Sony ATV Tunes LLC,
  2001/Sony ATV Songs LLC, 2001
Performed by Destiny's Child on the album *Survivor* (Columbia, 2001).

Born to Fly
Words and music by Marc Hummon, Sara Evans (pseudonym for Sara
  Schelske), and Darrell Scott
Chuck Wagon Gourmet Music, 2000/Famous Music Corp., 2000/
  Careers-BMG Music, 2000/Floyd's Dream Music, 2000/Tree
  Publishing, 2000
Performed by Sara Evans on the album *Born to Fly* (RCA, 2000).

Boss of Me
Words and music by John Flansburgh and John Linnell
Fox Film Music Corp., 2000/New Enterprises Music, 2000
Performed by They Might Be Giants as the theme song to the TV show
  Malcolm in the Middle. Also featured on the soundtrack album *Music
  From Malcolm in the Middle* (Restless, 2000). Won a Grammy
  Award for Best Song Written for a Motion Picture/Television, 2001.

Bouncing off the Ceiling (Upside Down)
Words and music by Gustav Jonsson, Tommy Pawlicki, and Markus
  Sepehrmanesh
Universal Polygram International Pub., 2000
Performed by the A*Teens on the album *Teen Spirit* (MCA, 2001).

Bow Wow (That's My Name)
Words and music by Snoop Dogg (pseudonym for Calvin Broadus),
  Bryan Cox, and Jermaine Dupri, music by George Clinton, Jr., Garry
  Shider, and David Spradley
EMI-April Music, 2000/So So Def Music, 2000/Bridgeport Music,
  2000/My Own Chit Publishing, 2000/Babyboys Little Pub Co, 2000
Performed by Lil' Bow Wow featuring Jermaine Dupri and Snoop Dogg
  on the album *Beware of Dog* (So So Def/Columbia, 2000).

The Boys Are Back in Town
Words and music by Stuart Duncan, Don Humphries, and Pat Enright
Obanyon Music, 1999
Performed by Patty Loveless on the album *Mountain Soul* (Epic, 2001).

Break 4 Love
Words and music by Vaughan Mason
Songs of Lastrada, 1987/Sony ATV Songs LLC, 1987
Covered by Peter Rauhofer and the Pet Shop Boys (a.k.a. the
  Collaboration) on the album *Essential Mix* (Full Frequency Range
  Recordings, 2001). Originally performed by Raze.

Break Ya Neck
Words and music by Dr. Dre (pseudonym for Andre Young), Michael
  Elizondo, Busta Rhymes (pseudonym for Trevor Smith), Scott Storch,
  Darrol Durant, and Roger Munroe
Ain't Nothing but Funkin', 2001/Blotter Music, 2001/Elvis Mambo
  Music, 2001/Music of Windswept, 2001/Scott Storch Music, 2001/
  Tziah Music, 2001
Performed by Busta Rhymes on the album *Genesis* (J Records, 2001).

Breakdown
Words and music by Hugo Ferreira, Matt Taul, Jesse Vest, and Todd
  Whitener
Cloud 29 Publishing, 2001/Oglirifica, 2001/WB Music Publishing, 2001/
  Cherryworks Music, 2001/Eight Inches Plus Publishing, 2001/Warner-
  Tamerlane Publishing, 2001
Performed by Tantric on the album *Tantric* (Maverick, 2001).

Bring on the Rain
Words and music by Helen Darling and Billy Montana
Bro N' Sis Music, 2000/Estes Park Music, 2000/Little Chatterbox
  Music, 2000
Performed by Jo Dee Messina featuring Tim McGraw on the album
  Burn (Curb, 2000). Nominated for a Grammy Award, Best Country
  Collaboration With Vocals, 2001.

Broken Vow
Words and music by Walter Afanasieff and Lara Fabian
Sony ATV Songs LLC, 2000/Wally World Music, 2000
Performed by Lara Fabian on the album *Lara Fabian* (Sony, 2000).

Burn
Words and music by Tina Arena, Pam Reswick, and Steve Werfel
EMI-Blackwood Music Inc., 1997/Reswick Songs, 1997/Stephen Werfel
  Songs, 1997
Covered by Jo Dee Messina on the album *Burn* (Curb, 2000). Originally
  performed by Tina Arena on the album *In Deep* (Columbia, 1997).

But for the Grace of God
Words and music by Charlotte Caffey, Jane Wiedlin, and Keith Urban
BMG Songs Inc., 1999/Stridgirl Music, 1999/Wiedwacker Music, 1999/
  Coburn Music, 1999

Performed by Keith Urban on the album *Keith Urban* (Capitol Nashville, 1999).

But I Do Love You
Words and music by Diane Warren
Realsongs, 1999
Performed by LeAnn Rimes on the album *I Need You* (Curb, 2001).

By Your Side
Words and music by Sade (pseudonym for Helen Adu), music by Paul Denman, Andrew Hale, and Stuart Matthewman
Sony ATV Songs LLC, 2000/Angel Music Ltd., 2000
Performed by Sade on the album *Lovers Rock* (Epic, 2000). Nominated for a Grammy Award, Best Female Pop Vocal Performance, 2001.

C

Can't Believe

Words and music by Jermaine Baxter, Sean Combs, Anthony Cruz, Tijuan Frampton, Mechalie Jamison, Michael Jones, Nasir Jones, Chris Taylor, Mario Winans, and Dr. Dre (pseudonym for Andre Young)

Ain't Nothing but Funkin', 2001/Black Ed Music, 2001/Dakoda House Music, 2001/EMI-April Music, 2001/Gloria's Boy Music, 2001/Hard Working Black Folks, 2001/Hot Heat Music, 2001/Ill Will Music, 2001/Justin Combs Publishing, 2001/Life's a Bitch Publishing, 2001/EMI-Blackwood Music Inc., 2001/Janice Combs Music/Marsky Music

Performed by Faith Evans featuring Carl Thomas. Initially released as a single; later featured on the album *Faithfully* (Bad Boy/Arista, 2001). Nominated for a Grammy Award, Best R&B Performance by a Duo or Group With Vocal, 2001.

Can't Deny It

Words and music by Nate Dogg (pseudonym for Nathaniel Hale), Fabolous (pseudonym for John Jackson), and Ricardo Thomas

Cyphercleff Music Publishing, 2001/EMI-April Music, 2001/J Brasco, 2001/Desert Storm Music, 2001/Nate Dogg Music, 2001

Performed by Fabolous featuring Nate Dogg on the album *Ghetto Fabolous* (Desert Storm/Elektra, 2001).

Carry On

Words and music by Pat Green and Walt Wilkins

Curb Congregation Songs, 1999/Greenhorse Music, 1999

Performed by Pat Green on the album *Three Days* (Republic/Universal, 2001). Originally featured on the album *Carry On* (Greenhorse, 2000).

Celos

Words and music by Palacios Jaen and Marc Anthony

Nueva Ventura Music, 2001/Sony ATV Tunes LLC, 2001

Performed by Marc Anthony on the album *Libre* (Sony, 2001).

Change the Game

Words by Jay-Z (pseudonym for Shawn Carter) and Beanie Sigel (pseudonym for Dwight Grant), words and music by Stephen Garrett, music by Rick Rock (pseudonym for Ricardo Thomas)

Cyphercleff Music Publishing, 2000/EMI-April Music, 2000/Herbilicious Music, 2000/Hitco South, 2000/Mo-Down Muzik, 2000/Shakur al Din Music, 2000/EMI-Blackwood Music Inc., 2000/Lil Lu Lu Publishing, 2000

Performed by Jay-Z featuring Beanie Sigel and Memphis Bleek on the album *The Dynasty: Roc la Familia* (Def Jam, 2000). Nominated for a Grammy Award, Best Rap Performance by a Duo or Group, 2001.

Cherry Lips (Go Baby Go!)

Words and music by Douglas Erickson, Shirley Manson, Steve Marker, and Butch Vig

Almo Music Corp., 2001/Deadarm Music, 2001/Irving Music Inc., 2001/ Vibe Crusher Music, 2001

Performed by Garbage on the album *Beautiful Garbage* (Interscope, 2001).

Choctaw Hayride

Music by Jerry Douglas

Nolivian Songs, 2001

Performed by Alison Krauss & Union Station on the album *New Favorite* (Rounder, 2001). Nominated for a Grammy Award, Best Country Instrumental Performance, 2001.

Chop Suey!

Words and music by Daron Malakian, words by Serj Tankian, music by Shavarsh Odadjian and John Dolmayan

Ddevil Music, 2001/Sony ATV Tunes LLC, 2001

Performed by System of a Down on the album *Toxicity* (American Recordings, 2001). Nominated for a Grammy Award, Best Metal Performance, 2001.

Clint Eastwood

Words and music by Damon Albarn, Jamie Hewlett, and Teren Jones

Happy Hemp Music, 2000/EMI-Blackwood Music Inc., 2000

Performed by Gorillaz featuring Del Tha Funkee Homosapien on the album *Gorillaz* (Virgin, 2001). Nominated for a Grammy Award, Best Rap Performance by a Duo or Group, 2001.

Cocky

Words and music by Frederick Beauregard, IV, Kid Rock (pseudonym for Robert Ritchie), and Uncle Kracker (pseudonym for Matthew Shafer)

Eighty Six Sixty Music, 2001/Gaje Music, 2001/Thirty Two Mile Music,

2001/Warner-Tamerlane Publishing, 2001
Performed by Kid Rock on the album *Cocky* (Lava/Atlantic, 2001).

Cold, Cold Heart
Words and music by Hank Williams
Acuff Rose Music, 1951/Rightsong Music, 1951
Covered by Lucinda Williams on the tribute album *Hank Williams: Timeless* (Lost Highway, 2001). Originally performed by Hank Williams. Nominated for a Grammy Award, Best Female Country Vocal Performance, 2001.

Colorful
Words and music by Donald Brown, Douglas Corella, Jeffrey Dunning, and Bradley Vander Ark
EMI-April Music, 2001/LMNO Pop Music, 2001
Performed by the Verve Pipe on the album *Underneath* (RCA, 2001).

Come a Little Closer
Words and music by Philip Douglas, Tony Marty, and Jennifer Sherrill
Baughnsongs, 2001/Charlie Monk Music, 2001/Curb Songs, 2001/Mick Hits Music, 2001/Curb Congregation Songs, 2001/Lil Strat Songs, 2001/Monkids Music, 2001
Performed by Lila McCann on the album *Complete* (Warner Bros., 2001).

Come What May
Words and music by David Baerwald
Almo Music Corp., 2001/TCF Music Publishing, 2001/Zen of Iniquity, 2001
Performed by Nicole Kidman and Ewan McGregor in the movie and on the soundtrack album *Moulin Rouge* (Interscope, 2001).

Complicated
Words and music by Carolyn Dawn Johnson and Shaye Smith
EMI-Blackwood Music Inc., 1999/Mark Alan Springer Music, 1999/April Blue Music, 1999/Blakemore Avenue Music, 1999/EMI-Full Keel Music, 1999
Performed by Carolyn Dawn Johnson on the album *Room With a View* (Arista Nashville, 2001).

Contagious
Words and music by R. Kelly
R. Kelly Publishing, 2001/Zomba Songs, 2001
Performed by the Isley Brothers on the album *Eternal* (DreamWorks, 2001). Nominated for a Grammy Award, Best R&B Performance by a Duo or Group With Vocal, 2001.

Control
Words and music by Wesley Scantlin and Brad Stewart

WB Music Publishing, 2001/EMI-April Music, 2001/Lithium Glass Music, 2001

Performed by Puddle of Mudd on the album *Come Clean* (Flawless/ Geffen, 2001).

Could It Be

Words and music by Bale'wa Muhammad, Charles Moore, Clifton Lighty, and Rashawn Worthen, music by Tony Hester

E Ballad Music, 2001/Hood Classic, 2001/I Want My Daddy's Records, 2001/Jahque Joints, 2001/Universal-Polygram International Tunes, 2001/EMI Longitude Music, 2001

Performed by Jaheim on the album *Ghetto Love* (Warner Bros., 2001).

Crawling

Words and music by Chester Bennington, Rob Bourdon, Brad Delson, Joseph Hahn, and Mike Shinoda

Zomba Enterprises, 2000/Chesterchaz Publishing, 2000/Zomba Songs, 2000/Nondisclosure Agreement Music, 2000/Rob Bourdon Music, 2000/Kenji Kobayashi Music, 2000

Performed by Linkin Park on the album *Hybrid Theory* (Warner Bros., 2000). Won a Grammy Award for Best Hard Rock Performance, 2001.

Crazy

Words and music by Darrell Allamby, Lincoln Browder, K-Ci (pseudonym for Cedric Hailey), and JoJo (pseudonym for Joel Hailey)

2000 Watts Music, 2000/Coral Rock Music Corp., 2000/LBN Publishing, 2000/WB Music Publishing, 2000

Performed by K-Ci and JoJo on the album *X* (MCA, 2000).

Cross the Border

Words and music by Holly Al-Baseer, Charles Hugo, Pharrell Williams, and Joel Witherspoon

Chase Chad Music, 2001/EMI-April Music, 2001/Fatima & Bara Outlet, 2001/Maine Money, 2001/EMI-Blackwood Music Inc., 2001/Waters of Nazareth Publishing, 2001

Performed by Philly's Most Wanted on the album *Get Down or Lay Down* (Atlantic, 2001).

Crystal

Words and music by Gillian Gilbert, Peter Hook, Stephen Morris, and Bernard Sumner

WB Music Publishing, 2001

Performed by New Order on the album *Get Ready* (Reprise, 2001).

D

Dance With Me
Words and music by Jason Boyd, Daron Jones, and Michael Keith
C Sills Publishing, 2001/Da 12 Music, 2001/EMI-April Music, 2001/
   Justin Combs Publishing, 2001
Performed by 112 on the album *Part III* (Bad Boy, 2001).

Danger (Been So Long)
Words and music by Charles Hugo, Mystikal (pseudonym for Michael
   Tyler), and Pharrell Williams
Chase Chad Music, 2000/EMI-April Music, 2000/Zomba Enterprises,
   2000/EMI-Blackwood Music Inc., 2000/Waters of Nazareth
   Publishing, 2000
Performed by Mystikal featuring Nivea on the album *Let's Get Ready*
   (Jive, 2000).

Days of the Week
Words and music by Dean DeLeo, Robert DeLeo, Eric Kretz, and Scott
   Weiland
EMI-April Music, 2001/Foxy Dead Girl Music, 2001/Milksongs, 2001
Performed by Stone Temple Pilots on the album *Shangri-la Dee Da*
   (Lava/Atlantic, 2001).

Defy You
Words and music by Bryan Holland
Underachiever Music, 2001
Performed by the Offspring on the movie soundtrack album *Orange
   County* (Columbia, 2001).

Diamond Dogs
Words and music by David Bowie (pseudonym for David Jones)
Chrysalis Music, 1974/Colgems-EMI Music, 1974/Jones Music America,
   1974
Covered by Beck on the movie soundtrack album *Moulin Rouge*
   (Interscope, 2001). Originally performed by Davie Bowie on the
   album *Diamond Dogs* (RCA, 1974).

Didn't Cha Know
Words and music by Erykah Badu and James Yancey
BMG Songs Inc., 2000/Divine Pimp Music, 2000/EPHCY Publishing,
   2000
Performed by Erykah Badu on the album *Mama's Gun* (Motown, 2000).
   Nominated for a Grammy Award, Best R&B Song, 2001.

Didn't Leave Nobody but the Baby
Words and music by Henry Burnett and Gillian Welch, music by Alan
   Lomax and Sidney Carter
Henry Burnett Music, 2000/Irving Music Inc., 2000/Global Jukebox
   Publishing, 2000/Say Uncle Music, 2000
Performed by Emmylou Harris, Alison Krauss, and Gillian Welch in the
   movie and on the soundtrack album *O Brother, Where Art Thou?*
   (Lost Highway, 2000). Nominated for a Grammy Award, Best
   Country Collaboration With Vocals, 2001.

Differences
Words and music by Ginuwine (pseudonym for Elgin Lumpkin) and
   Troy Oliver
Black Fountain Music, 2001/Golddaddy Music, 2001/Milk Chocolate
   Factory, 2001/Sony ATV Tunes LLC, 2001
Performed by Ginuwine on the album *The Life* (Epic, 2001).

Dig In
Words and music by Lenny Kravitz
Miss Bessie Music, 2001
Performed by Lenny Kravitz on the album *Lenny* (Virgin, 2001). Won a
   Grammy Award for Best Male Rock Vocal Performance, 2001.

Digital Love
Words and music by Thomas Bangalter, Guy de Homem-Christo,
   Anthony Moore, and Carlos Sosa
Mycenae Music Publishing Co., 2000/Sneaka Rican Music, 2000/Zomba
   Songs, 2000
Performed by Daft Punk on the album *Discovery* (Virgin, 2001).

Dirty Mind
Music by Jeff Beck, Aidan Love, and Andy Wright
Songs of Windswept Pacific, 2001/Windswept Music, 2001
Performed by Jeff Beck on the album *You Had It Coming* (Epic, 2001).
   Won a Grammy Award for Best Rock Instrumental Performance,
   2001.

Disciple
Words and music by Kerry King, music by Jeffery Hanneman
Molosser Music, 2001/Pennemunde Music, 2001

Performed by Slayer on the album *God Hates Us All* (American, 2001). Nominated for a Grammy Award, Best Metal Performance, 2001.

Dog in Heat
Words and music by Missy Elliott, Timbaland (pseudonym for Timothy Mosley), Redman (pseudonym for Reggie Noble), and Method Man (pseudonym for Clifford Smith)
Careers-BMG Music, 2001/Wu-Tang Publishing, 2001/Mass Confusion Productions, 2001/Virginia Beach Music, 2001/Funky Noble Productions, 2001
Performed by Missy Elliott featuring Redman and Method Man on the album *Miss E . . . So Addictive* (The Gold Mind/Elektra, 2001).

Dollaz, Drank & Dank
Words by Mr. Short Khop (pseudonym for Lionel Hunt), music by Kevin Gilliam
Always Thinkin, 2001/Show You How Daddy Ball Music, 2001
Performed by Mr. Short Khop featuring Kokane on the album *Da Khop Shop* (TVT, 2001).

Done Got Old
Words and music by Junior Kimbrough
Music River Publishing, 1993
Performed by Buddy Guy on the album *Sweet Tea* (Jive, 2001).
    Originally performed by Junior Kimbrough.

Don't Happen Twice
Words and music by Curtis Lance (pseudonym for Curtis Hickman) and Tom McHugh
EMI-April Music, 2000/Gotta Groove Music, 2000/Copyright Net Music, 2000/Mcmore Music, 2000
Performed by Kenny Chesney on the album *Greatest Hits* (BNA, 2000).

Don't Let Me Be Lonely Tonight
Words and music by James Taylor
EMI-Blackwood Music Inc., 1973/Country Road Music, 1973
Covered by Michael Brecker featuring James Taylor on the album *Nearness of You: The Ballad Book* (Verve, 2001). Originally performed by James Taylor on the album *One Man Dog* (Warner Bros., 1972). Won a Grammy Award for Best Male Pop Vocal Performance, 2001.

Don't Talk
Words and music by Jon B (pseudonym for Jonathan Buck)
Sony ATV Songs LLC, 2001/Vibzelect, 2001/Yab Yum Music, 2001
Performed by Jon B on the album *Pleasures U Like* (Epic, 2001).

Don't Tell Me
Words and music by Mirwais (pseudonym for Mirwais Ahmadzai),

Madonna (pseudonym for Madonna Ciccone), and Joe Henry
True North Music, 2000/WB Music Publishing, 2000/Webo Girl
  Publishing, 2000/Warner-Tamerlane Publishing, 2000
Performed by Madonna on the album *Music* (Maverick/Warner Bros.,
  2000). Nominated for a Grammy Award, Best Short Form Music
  Video, 2001.

Down From Dover
Words and music by Dolly Parton
Velvet Apple Music, 1969
Performed by Dolly Parton on the album *Little Sparrow* (Sugar Hill,
  2001). Originally featured on the album *The Fairest of Them All*
  (RCA, 1970).

Downtime
Words and music by Phillip Coleman and Carolyn Dawn Johnson
Blakemore Avenue Music, 2000/EMI-Full Keel Music, 2000/Gravitron
  Music, 2000
Performed by Jo Dee Messina on the album *Burn* (Curb, 2000).

Dream On
Words and music by Martin Gore
EMI-Blackwood Music Inc., 2001/EMI Music Publishing, 2001
Performed by Depeche Mode on the album *Exciter* (Mute/Reprise,
  2001).

Drinkin' Wine Spo-Dee-O-Dee
Words and music by Granville McGhee and J. Williams
Universal-MCA Music Publishing, 1953
Covered by the Howling Diablos featuring Kid Rock on the album
  Good Rockin' Tonight: The Legacy of Sun Records (Sire, 2001).
  Originally performed by Jerry Lee Lewis.

Drops of Jupiter (Tell Me)
Words and music by Pat Monahan, Jim Stafford, Scott Underwood,
  Charlie Colin, and Rob Hotchkiss
Blue Lamp Music, 2001/EMI-Blackwood Music Inc., 2001/Wunderwood
  Music, 2001
Performed by Train on the album *Drops of Jupiter* (Columbia, 2001).
  Won a Grammy Award for Best Rock Song, 2001. Nominated for
  Grammy Awards, Best Rock Performance by a Duo or Group With
  Vocal, 2001, Record of the Year, 2001, and Song of the Year, 2001.

Drowning
Words and music by Andreas Carlsson, Linda Thompson, and Rami
  Yacoub
Zomba Enterprises, 2001/Brandon Brody Music, 2001/Warner-
  Tamerlane Publishing, 2001

Performed by the Backstreet Boys on the album *The Hits: Chapter One* (Jive, 2001).

Duck and Run

Words and music by Brad Arnold, Christopher Henderson, and Matthew Roberts, music by Robert Harrell

Escatawpa Songs, 2000/Songs of Universal, 2000

Performed by 3 Doors Down on the album *The Better Life* (Republic/Universal, 2000).

E

E.I.
Words by Nelly (pseudonym for Cornell Haynes), music by Jason
    Epperson
BMG Songs Inc., 2000/Jay E's Basement, 2000/Universal-MCA Music
    Publishing, 2000
Performed by Nelly on the album *Country Grammar* (Universal, 2000).

Elevation
Words and music by Bono (pseudonym for Paul Hewson), music by The
    Edge (pseudonym for David Evans), Larry Mullen, Jr., and Adam
    Clayton
Universal Polygram International Pub., 2000
Performed by U2 on the album *All That You Can't Leave Behind*
    (Interscope, 2000). Won a Grammy Award for Best Rock
    Performance by a Duo or Group With Vocal, 2001. Nominated for a
    Grammy Award, Best Rock Song, 2001.

Elvis Presley Blues
Words and music by Gillian Welch and David Rawlings
Cracklin' Music, 2001/Irving Music Inc., 2001
Performed by Gillian Welch on the album *Time (The Revelator)* (Acony,
    2001).

Emotion
Words and music by Barry Gibb and Robin Gibb
Gibb Brothers Music, 1977
Covered by Destiny's Child on the album *Survivor* (Columbia, 2001).
    Originally performed by Samantha Sang on the album *Emotion*
    (Private Stock, 1978).

Emotional
Words and music by Fredrik Thomander and Anders Wikstrom
Jimmie Fun Music, 2001
Performed by Mikaila on the album *Mikaila* (Island, 2001).

Emotional
Words and music by Carl Thomas, Mario Winans, and K. Hickson
Thom Tunes, 2000/EMI-Blackwood Music Inc., 2000/Butter Jinx Music,
    2000/Yellow Man Music, 2000
Performed by Carl Thomas on the album *Emotional* (Bad Boy, 2000).

Enjoy Yourself
Words and music by Kobie Brown, Keir Gist, Christopher Liggio, and
    Tanya Von
Divine Mill Music, 2001/WB Music Publishing, 2001/Beat Wise Music,
    2001/Proceed Music, 2001
Performed by Allure on the album *Sunny Days* (MCA, 2001).

Essence
Words and music by Lucinda Williams
Lucy Jones Music, 2001/Warner-Tamerlane Publishing, 2001
Performed by Lucinda Williams on the album *Essence* (Lost Highway,
    2001). Nominated for a Grammy Award, Best Female Pop Vocal
    Performance, 2001.

Every Day
Words and music by Damon Johnson and John Shanks
EMI-Virgin Music, 2001/Line One Publishing, 2001/Little Miss Music,
    2001
Performed by Stevie Nicks on the album *Trouble in Shangri-la* (Reprise,
    2001).

Every Other Time
Words and music by Rich Cronin, Kenneth Gioia, and Michael
    Goodman
Chrysalis Music, 2001/Marty Bags Music, 2001/Chrysalis Songs, 2001/
    Noise Dog Productions, 2001
Performed by LFO on the album *Life Is Good* (J Records, 2001).

(Everything I Do) I Do It for You
Words and music by Bryan Adams, Michael Kamen, and Robert John
    Lange
2855 Music, 1991/Almo Music Corp., 1991/Miracle Creek Music, 1991/
    Zomba Enterprises, 1991/Zachary Creek Music, 1991
Covered by Neal Schon on the album *Voice* (Higher Octave, 2001).
    Originally performed by Bryan Adams on the movie soundtrack
    album *Robin Hood: Prince of Thieves* (Morgan Creek, 1991). Also
    featured on Adams' album *Waking Up the Neighbours* (A&M, 1991).

Everywhere
Words and music by Michelle Branch and John Shanks
EMI-Virgin Music, 2001/I'm With the Band Music, 2001/Line One
    Publishing, 2001

Performed by Michelle Branch on the album *The Spirit Room* (Maverick, 2001).

Extra Ordinary
Words and music by Kevin Griffin
Tentative Music, 2001
Performed by Better Than Ezra featuring DJ Swamp on the album *Closer* (Beyond, 2001).

F

Fade
Words and music by John April, Aaron Lewis, Michael Mushok, and
Jonathan Wysocki
Greenfund, 2000/I'm Nobody Music, 2000/My Blue Car Music, 2000/
Pimp Yug, 2000/WB Music Publishing, 2000
Performed by Staind on the album *Break the Cycle* (Flip/Elektra, 2001).

Fallin'
Words and music by Alicia Keys (pseudonym for Alicia Augello-Cook)
EMI-April Music, 2001
Performed by Alicia Keys on the album *Songs in A Minor* (J Records,
2001). Won Grammy Awards. Nominated for a Grammy Award,
Record of the Year, 2001.

Falling for the First Time
Words and music by Steven Page and Ed Robertson
WB Music Publishing, 2000
Performed by the Barenaked Ladies on the album *Maroon* (Reprise,
2000). Also featured on the TV soundtrack album *Music From
Malcolm in the Middle* (Restless, 2000).

Family Affair
Words and music by Dr. Dre (pseudonym for Andre Young), Luchana
Lodge, Asiah Lous, Bruce Miller, Mary J. Blige, Melvin Bradford,
Michael Elizondo, and Camara Kambon
Asiahtown Ent., 2001/Colorscapes Publishing, 2001/Luchi Publishing,
2001/Universal-MCA Music Publishing, 2001/Elvis Mambo Music,
2001/Blotter Music, 2001/Mary J. Blige Music, 2001/Music of
Windswept, 2001/Ain't Nothing but Funkin', 2001
Performed by Mary J. Blige on the album *No More Drama* (MCA,
2001). Nominated for a Grammy Award, Best Female R&B Vocal
Performance, 2001.

Fast Lane
Words and music by Bilal (pseudonym for Bilal Oliver), James Mtume,

Damu Mtume, Dr. Dre (pseudonym for Andre Young), and Mike City (pseudonym for Michael Flowers)
Mike City Music, 2001/Mtume Music, 2001/Ain't Nothing but Funkin', 2001/WB Music Publishing, 2001/Jazzmen Publishing, 2001
Performed by Bilal featuring Dr. Dre and Jadakiss on the album *1st Born Second* (Interscope, 2001).

Fat Lip
Words and music by Dave Baksh, Stevo 32 (pseudonym for Steve Jocz), Greig Nori, and Deryck Whibley
Chrysalis Music, 2001/EMI-April Music, 2001
Performed by Sum 41 on the album *All Killer No Filler* (Island, 2001).

Feelin' on Yo Booty
Words and music by R. Kelly
R. Kelly Publishing, 2000/Zomba Songs, 2000
Performed by R. Kelly on the album *TP-2.com* (Jive, 2000).

Fiesta
Words and music by R. Kelly
R. Kelly Publishing, 2000/Zomba Songs, 2000
Performed by R. Kelly featuring Jay-Z, Boo, and Gotti on the album *TP-2.com* (Jive, 2000).

Fight Music
Words and music by Von Carlisle, Michael Elizondo, DeShaun Holton, Rufus Johnson, Eminem (pseudonym for Marshall Mathers), Ondre Moore, Denaun Porter, and Dr. Dre (pseudonym for Andre Young)
Ain't Nothing but Funkin', 2001/Blotter Music, 2001/Derty Werks, 2001/Elvis Mambo Music, 2001/EMI-April Music, 2001/Idiotic Biz, 2001/Music of Windswept, 2001/Runyon Ave, 2001/Swifty McVay Publishing, 2001/Eight Mile Style Music, 2001/EMI-Blackwood Music Inc., 2001/Ensign Music, 2001
Performed by D12 on the album *Devil's Night* (Shady/Interscope, 2001).

Fill Me In
Words and music by Craig David and Mark Hill
Music of Windswept, 2000/WB Music Publishing, 2000
Performed by Craig David on the album *Born to Do It* (Wildstar/Atlantic, 2001). Nominated for a Grammy Award, Best Male Pop Vocal Performance, 2001.

Flavor of the Weak
Words and music by Stacy Jones
BMG Songs Inc., 2001/Disciples of Judra, 2001
Performed by American Hi-Fi on the album *American Hi-Fi* (Island, 2001).

Fly Away From Here
Words and music by Todd Chapman and Martin Frederiksen
EMI-Blackwood Music Inc., 2001/Pearl White Music, 2001/Todski
    Music, 2001/Warner-Tamerlane Publishing, 2001
Performed by Aerosmith on the album *Just Push Play* (Columbia,
    2001). Nominated for a Grammy Award, Best Short Form Music
    Video, 2001.

Foggy Mountain Breakdown
Music by Earl Scruggs
APRS Music, 1950
Performed by Earl Scruggs and Friends featuring Glen Duncan, Randy
    Scruggs, Steve Martin, Vince Gill, Marty Stuart, Gary Scruggs, Albert
    Lee, Paul Shaffer, Jerry Douglas, and Leon Russell on the album *Earl
    Scruggs and Friends* (MCA Nashville, 2001). Originally performed
    by Flatt and Scruggs. Won a Grammy Award for Best Country
    Instrumental Performance, 2001.

Follow Me
Words and music by Michael Bradford and Uncle Kracker (pseudonym
    for Matthew Shafer)
Chunky Style Music, 2000/Seven Peaks Music, 2000/Gaje Music, 2000
Performed by Uncle Kracker on the album *Double Wide* (Lava/Atlantic,
    2000).

Forever
Words and music by Frederick Beauregard, IV, Kid Rock (pseudonym
    for Robert Ritchie), and Uncle Kracker (pseudonym for Matthew
    Shafer)
Eighty Six Sixty Music, 2001/Gaje Music, 2001/Thirty Two Mile Music,
    2001
Performed by Kid Rock on the album *Cocky* (Lava/Atlantic, 2001).

Freedom
Words and music by Paul McCartney
MPL Communications, 2001
Performed by Paul McCartney on the benefit album *The Concert for
    New York City* (Sony, 2001). Also featured on McCartney's album
    Driving Rain (Capitol, 2001).

From a Lover to a Friend
Words and music by Paul McCartney
MPL Communications, 2001
Performed by Paul McCartney on the album *Driving Rain* (Capitol,
    2001).

G

Gasoline Dreams
Words and music by Andre Benjamin, Willie Knighton, Antwan Patton, and David Sheats
Dungeon Rat Music, 2000/Gnat Booty Music, 2000/Goodie Mob Music, 2000
Performed by Outkast featuring Khujo Goodie on the album *Stankonia* (LaFace/Arista, 2000).

Georgia
Words and music by Carolyn Dawn Johnson and Thomas Verges
April Blue Music, 1999/Blakemore Avenue Music, 1999/EMI-Full Keel Music, 1999/EMI Longitude Music, 1999/Wedgewood Avenue Music, 1999
Performed by Carolyn Dawn Johnson. Initially released as a single (Arista Nashville, 2000); later featured on the album *Room With a View* (Arista Nashville, 2001).

Get It Up (The Feeling)
Words and music by Arnthor Birgisson, Ernest Isley, Marvin Isley, O'Kelly Isley, Ronald Isley, Rudolph Isley, Christopher Jasper, Christian Karlsson, Patrick Tucker, and Ultra Nate Wyche
Bovina Music, 2001/EMI-April Music, 2001
Performed by Ultra Nate on the album *Stranger Than Fiction* (Strictly Rhythm, 2001).

Get to Know Ya
Words and music by Maxwell
Muszewell Music, 2001/Sony ATV Tunes LLC, 2001
Performed by Maxwell on the album *Now* (Columbia, 2001).

Get Over Yourself
Words and music by Matthew Gerrard, John Keller, and Michele Vice
G Matt Music, 2001/WB Music Publishing, 2001/Checkerman Music, 2001/Dayspring Music, 2001
Performed by Eden's Crush on the album *Popstars* (Sire, 2001).

Get the Party Started
Words and music by Linda Perry
Famous Music Corp., 2001/Stuck in the Throat, 2001
Performed by Pink on the album *M!ssundaztood* (Arista, 2001).

Get Right With God
Words and music by Lucinda Williams
Lucy Jones Music, 2001/Warner-Tamerlane Publishing, 2001
Performed by Lucinda Williams on the album *Essence* (Lost Highway,
    2001). Won a Grammy Award for Best Female Rock Vocal
    Performance, 2001.

Get Ur Freak On
Words and music by Missy Elliott and Timbaland (pseudonym for
    Timothy Mosley)
Mass Confusion Productions, 2001/Virginia Beach Music, 2001/WB
    Music Publishing, 2001
Performed by Missy Elliott on the album *Miss E . . . So Addictive* (The
    Gold Mind/Elektra, 2001). Won a Grammy Award for Best Rap Solo
    Performance, 2001. Nominated for a Grammy Award, Best R&B
    Song, 2001.

Gets Me Through
Words and music by Ozzy Osbourne and Tim Palmer
EMI-Virgin Music, 2001/TP Songs, 2001/Monowise Ltd., 2001/Parker
    Music, 2001
Performed by Ozzy Osbourne on the album *Down to Earth* (Epic,
    2001).

Ghost of You and Me
Words and music by Jonathan Lind and Richard Page
Little Dume Music, 1995/Big Mystique Music, 1995/EMI-Virgin Music,
    1995
Covered by BBMak on the album *Sooner or Later* (Hollywood, 2000).
    Originally performed by Curtis Stigers on the album *Time Was*
    (Arista, 1995).

Girls, Girls, Girls
Words and music by Jay-Z (pseudonym for Shawn Carter), Tom Brock,
    Robert Relf, Justin Smith, Barry Bailey, Barry Belton, Charles
    Fleming, Larry Miller, and Reginald Payne
EMI-Blackwood Music Inc., 2001/Lil Lu Lu Publishing, 2001/
    Unichappell Music Inc., 2001
Performed by Jay-Z featuring Q-Tip, Slick Rick, and Biz Markie on the
    album *The Blueprint* (Def Jam, 2001).

Giving In
Words and music by Mark Chavez, Dave DeRoo, Tim Fluckey, Kris

Kohls, and Mike Ransom
Kohlslaw Music, 2001/Marky Chavez Publishing, 2001/Rock the Mike
Music, 2001/Warner-Tamerlane Publishing, 2001/De Roo Toons
Music, 2001/Klown County, 2001
Performed by Adema on the album *Adema* (Arista, 2001).

God Gave Me Everything
Words and music by Mick Jagger and Lenny Kravitz
Mick Jagger Music, 2001/Miss Bessie Music, 2001
Performed by Mick Jagger featuring Lenny Kravitz on the album
Goddess in the Doorway (Virgin, 2001).

Gone
Words and music by Wade Robson and Justin Timberlake
Tennman Tunes, 2001/Wajero Music, 2001
Performed by *NSYNC on the album *Celebrity* (Jive, 2001). Nominated
for a Grammy Award, Best Pop Performance by a Duo or Group
With Vocal, 2001.

Gonna Make You Love Me
Words and music by Ryan Adams
Barland Music, 2001
Performed by Ryan Adams on the album *Gold* (Lost Highway, 2001).

A Good Day to Run
Words and music by Bobby Tomberlin and Darryl Worley
EMI-Blackwood Music Inc., 2001/Hatley Creek Music, 2000/Mike Curb
Music, 2000
Performed by Darryl Worley on the album *Hard Rain Don't Last*
(DreamWorks, 2000).

Greed
Words and music by Sully (pseudonym for Salvatore Erna)
Meeengya Music, 2000
Performed by Godsmack on the album *Awake* (Republic/Universal,
2000).

Grimey
Words and music by Charles Hugo, Noreaga (pseudonym for Victor
Santiago), and Pharrell Williams
Chase Chad Music, 2001/EMI-April Music, 2001/EMI-Blackwood
Music Inc., 2001/Jose Luis Gotcha Music, 2001/Waters of Nazareth
Publishing, 2001
Performed by Noreaga on the various-artists album *Violator: The Album,
V2.0* (Violator/Loud, 2001).

Grown Men Don't Cry
Words and music by Tom Douglas and Steve Seskin
Larga Vista Music, 2001/Scarlet Rain Music, 2001/Tree Publishing,

2001
Performed by Tim McGraw on the album *Set This Circus Down* (Curb, 2001). Nominated for a Grammy Award, Best Male Country Vocal Performance, 2001.

H

Hanging by a Moment
Words and music by Jason Wade
Cherry River Music, 2000/G Chills Music, 2000
Performed by Lifehouse on the album *No Name Face* (DreamWorks, 2000).

Hard to Explain
Words and music by Julian Casablancas
The Strokes Band Music, 2001
Performed by the Strokes on the album *Is This It* (RCA, 2001).

Hash Pipe
Words and music by Rivers Cuomo
E. O. Smith Music, 2001
Performed by Weezer on the album *Weezer* (Geffen, 2001).

He Loves U Not
Words and music by David Frank, Stephen Kipner, and Pamela Sheyne
EMI-April Music, 2000/Griff Griff Music, 2000/Stephen A. Kipner Music, 2000/Appletree Songs, 2000
Performed by Dream on the album *It Was All a Dream* (Bad Boy, 2001).

Heard It All Before
Words and music by Sunshine Anderson, Mike City (pseudonym for Michael Flowers), and Rayshawn Sherrer
Pinkys Playhouse, 2001/Mike City Music, 2001/Soulife Copyright Holdings, 2001/Warner-Tamerlane Publishing, 2001
Performed by Sunshine Anderson on the album *Your Woman* (Atlantic, 2001).

Here's to the Night
Words and music by James Collins, Anthony Fagenson, and Jonathan Siebels
Fake and Jaded Music, 2000/Less Than Zero Music, 2000/Southfield

Road Music, 2000
Performed by Eve 6 on the album *Horrorscope* (RCA, 2000).

Hero
Words and music by Paul Barry, Enrique Iglesias, and Mark Taylor
EMI-April Music, 2001/Enrique Iglesias Music, 2001/Right Bank Music,
2001/Seven Peaks Music, 2001
Performed by Enrique Iglesias on the album *Escape* (Interscope, 2001).

Hey Baby
Words and music by Gwen Stefani, Thomas Dumont, Tony Kanal, and
Rodney Price
Universal-MCA Music Publishing, 2001/World of the Dolphin Music,
2001
Performed by No Doubt on the album *Rock Steady* (Interscope, 2001).

Hidden Place
Words and music by Bjork (pseudonym for Bjork Gudmundsdottir)
Universal Polygram International Pub., 2001
Performed by Bjork on the album *Vespertine* (Elektra, 2001).

Hide U
Words and music by Darren Beale, Mark Morrison, and Sian Evans
Tairona Songs Ltd., 2000
Covered by Suzanne Palmer. Released as a single (Star 69, 2001).
  Originally performed by Kosheen.

High Falls
Music by Dickey Betts
Forrest Richard Betts Music, 1975/Unichappell Music Inc., 1975
Performed by the Allman Brothers Band on the album *Peakin' at the
Beacon* (Epic/550, 2000). Originally performed on the album *Win,
Lose, or Draw* (Capricorn, 1975). Nominated for a Grammy Award,
Best Rock Instrumental Performance, 2001.

Hit 'Em Up Style (Oops!)
Words and music by Dallas Austin
Cyptron Music, 2001/EMI-Blackwood Music Inc., 2001
Performed by Blu Cantrell on the album *So Blu* (Arista, 2001).
  Nominated for Grammy Awards, Best Female R&B Vocal
  Performance, 2001, and Best R&B Song, 2001.

Honest With Me
Words and music by Bob Dylan (pseudonym for Robert Zimmerman)
Special Rider Music, 2001
Performed by Bob Dylan on the album *Love and Theft* (Columbia,
2001). Nominated for a Grammy Award, Best Male Rock Vocal
Performance, 2001.

Hotel Yorba
Words and music by Jack White
Peppermint Stripe Music, 2001
Performed by the White Stripes on the album *White Blood Cells*
   (Sympathy for the Record Industry, 2001).

How Does It Make You Feel
Words and music by Barbier Dunckel and Nicolas Godin
Revolvair Sarl, 2001/Songs of Universal, 2001
Performed by Air on the album *10,000 Hz Legend* (Astralwerks, 2001).

How You Remind Me
Words and music by Chad Kroeger, Michael Kroeger, Ryan Peake, and
   Ryan Vikedal
Warner-Tamerlane Publishing, 2001
Performed by Nickelback on the album *Silver Side Up* (Roadrunner,
   2001).

The Humpty Dumpty Love Song
Words and music by Francis Healy
Sony ATV Songs LLC, 2001
Performed by Travis on the album *The Invisible Band* (Epic, 2001).

I

I Am a Man of Constant Sorrow

Traditional

Performed by the fictional band the Soggy Bottom Boys (Dan Tyminski, Harley Allen, Pat Enright) in the movie and on the soundtrack album *O Brother, Where Art Thou?* (Lost Highway, 2000). Won a Grammy Award for Best Country Collaboration With Vocals, 2001.

I Can't Deny It

Words and music by Gregg Alexander and Richard Nowels

Keepin It Real How Bout You Music, 2000/EMI-April Music, 2000/Future Furniture, 2000/Grosse Point Harlem Publishing, 2000

Performed by Rod Stewart on the album *Human* (Atlantic, 2000).

I Could Not Ask for More

Words and music by Diane Warren

Realsongs, 1999

Covered by Sara Evans on the album *Born to Fly* (RCA, 2000). Originally performed by Edwin McCain on the movie soundtrack album *Message in a Bottle* (Atlantic, 1999) and later featured on McCain's album *Messenger* (Atlantic, 1999).

I Cry

Words and music by Ja Rule (pseudonym for Jeffrey Atkins), Irv Gotti (pseudonym for Irving Lorenzo), Cynthia Loving, and Robin Mays, music by Kenneth Gamble and Leon Huff

6 Mo Shots Music, 2000/DJ Irv Publishing, 2000/Ensign Music, 2000/White Rhino Music, 2000/Mo Loving Music, 2000

Performed by Ja Rule featuring Lil' Mo on the album *Rule 3:36* (Def Jam, 2000).

I Did It

Words and music by David Matthews and Glen Ballard

Aerostation Corp., 2000/Colden Grey Ltd., 2000/Universal-MCA Music Publishing, 2000

Performed by the Dave Matthews Band on the album *Everyday* (RCA, 2001).

I Didn't Mean to Turn You On
Words and music by James Harris, III and Terry Lewis
Avant Garde Music Publishing, 1984/EMI-April Music, 1984/Flyte Tyme Tunes, 1984
Covered by Mariah Carey on the movie soundtrack album *Glitter* (Virgin, 2001). Originally performed by Cherrelle on the album *Fragile* (Tabu, 1984).

I Do!!
Words and music by Toya (pseudonym for LaToya Rodriguez), T. Beale, Harold Guy, R. Herbert, and C. Mack
Phat Nasty, Pensacola, 2001/EMI Longitude Music, 2001/MCA Music Publishing, 2001/Teron Beal Songs, 2001/Toy Toy Music, 2001/ Shack Suga Entertainment, 2001/Mijohkel, 2001/J Music for Stixx and Tones, 2001
Performed by Toya on the album *Toya* (Arista, 2001).

I Dreamed About Mama Last Night
Words and music by Fred Rose
Milene Music, 1949
Covered by Johnny Cash on the tribute album *Hank Williams: Timeless* (Lost Highway, 2001). Originally performed by Hank Williams. Nominated for a Grammy Award, Best Male Country Vocal Performance, 2001.

I Feel Loved
Words and music by Martin Gore
EMI-Blackwood Music Inc., 2001/EMI Music Publishing, 2001
Performed by Depeche Mode on the album *Exciter* (Mute/Reprise, 2001). Nominated for a Grammy Award, Best Dance Recording, 2001.

I Just Wanna Love U (Give It 2 Me)
Words by Jay-Z (pseudonym for Shawn Carter), music by Deric Angelettie, Mason Betha, Sean Combs, Charles Hugo, James Johnson, Todd Shaw, Christopher Walker, Notorious B.I.G. (pseudonym for Christopher Wallace), and Pharrell Williams
Chase Chad Music, 2000/EMI-April Music, 2000/Jobete Music Co., 2000/Deric Angelettie Music, 2000/EMI-Blackwood Music Inc., 2000/ Lil Lu Lu Publishing, 2000/Srand Music, 2000/Waters of Nazareth Publishing, 2000/Wind Tiger Music, 2000/Zomba Songs, 2000
Performed by Jay-Z on the album *The Dynasty: Roc la Familia* (Def Jam, 2000).

I Know
Words and music by Warryn Campbell, Harold Lilly, John Smith, Notasha Squire, and Tiffany Squire
Dango Music, 2000/EMI-April Music, 2000/Nyrraw Music, 2000/EMI-Blackwood Music Inc., 2000/Uncle Bobby Music, 2000
Performed by Sunday on the album *Sunday* (Better Place/Capitol, 2000).

I Like Them Girls
Words and music by Damon Thomas, Harvey Mason, Johnnie Newt, and Phillip White
Valentine's Day Songs, 2001/Warner-Tamerlane Publishing, 2001/First Avenue Music Ltd., 2001/Demis Hot Songs, 2001/E Two Music, 2001/EMI-April Music, 2001/Smooth As Silk Publishing, 2001/Plaything Music, 2001
Performed by Tyrese on the album *2000 Watts* (RCA, 2001).

I Wanna Be Bad
Words and music by Brian Kierulf, Joshua Schwartz, and Willa Ford (pseudonym for Amanda Lee Williford)
Mcud Music, 2001/Zomba Enterprises, 2001/Kierulf Songs, 2001/Mugsy Boy Publishing, 2001/Zomba Songs, 2001
Performed by Willa Ford on the album *Willa Was Here* (Lava/Atlantic, 2001).

I Wanna Talk About Me
Words and music by Bobby Braddock
Tree Publishing, 2001
Performed by Toby Keith on the album *Pull My Chain* (DreamWorks, 2001).

I Want to Be in Love
Words and music by Melissa Etheridge
M L E Music, 2001
Performed by Melissa Etheridge on the album *Skin* (Island, 2001). Nominated for a Grammy Award, Best Female Rock Vocal Performance, 2001.

I Want Love
Words by Bernard Taupin, music by Elton John (pseudonym for Reginald Dwight)
Warner-Tamerlane Publishing, 2001/Wretched Music, 2001
Performed by Elton John on the album *Songs From the West Coast* (Rocket/Universal, 2001). Nominated for a Grammy Award, Best Male Pop Vocal Performance, 2001.

I Want You to Want Me
Words and music by Rick Nielsen
Adult Music, 1977/Screen Gems-EMI Music Inc., 1977

Covered by Dwight Yoakam on the album *Tomorrow's Sounds Today* (Reprise, 2000). Originally performed by Cheap Trick on the album *In Color* (Epic, 1977).

I Would've Loved You Anyway
Words and music by Mary Danna and Troy Verges
Dannasongs, 2001/Ensign Music, 2001/Songs of Universal, 2001
Performed by Trisha Yearwood on the album *Inside Out* (MCA Nashville, 2001). Nominated for a Grammy Award, Best Female Country Vocal Performance, 2001.

If I Didn't Have You
Words and music by Randy Newman
Pixar Talking Pictures, 2001/Disney Music Publishing, 2001
Performed by Randy Newman on the movie soundtrack album *Monsters, Inc.* (Disney, 2001). Won an Academy Award for Best Original Song, 2001.

If I Fall You're Going Down With Me
Words and music by Matraca Berg and Annie Roboff
Almo Music Corp., 1999/Anwa Music, 1999
Performed by the Dixie Chicks on the album *Fly* (Monument, 1999).

If My Heart Had Wings
Words and music by Annie Roboff and James Knobloch
Almo Music Corp., 1999/Anwa Music, 1999/J. Fred Knobloch Music, 1999
Performed by Faith Hill on the album *Breathe* (Warner Bros., 1999).

If You Can Do Anything Else
Words and music by William Livsey and Donald Schlitz
New Don Songs, 2000/New Hayes Music, 2000/Billy Livsey Music, 2000/EMI-Blackwood Music Inc., 2000
Performed by George Strait on the album *George Strait* (MCA Nashville, 2000).

I'm Already There
Words and music by Gary Baker, Richie McDonald, and Frank Myers
Josh Nick Music, 1999/Swear By It Music, 1999/Zomba Enterprises, 1999/Tree Publishing, 1999
Performed by Lonestar on the album *I'm Already There* (BNA, 2001). Nominated for Grammy Awards, Best Country Performance by a Duo/Group With Vocal, 2001, and Best Country Song, 2001.

I'm a Believer
Words and music by Neil Diamond
Foray Music, 1966/Stonebridge Music, 1966
Covered by Smash Mouth in the movie and on the soundtrack album *Shrek* (DreamWorks, 2001). Later featured on the Smash Mouth

album *Smash Mouth* (Interscope, 2001). Originally performed by the Monkees.

I'm In
Words and music by Radney Foster and Georgia Middleman
On My Mind Music, 1998/St. Julien Music, 1998
Covered by the Kinleys on the album *II* (Epic, 2000). Originally performed by Radney Foster on the album *See What You Want to See* (Arista Nashville, 1999).

I'm Just Talkin' About Tonight
Words and music by Scotty Emerick and Toby Keith (pseudonym for Toby Covel)
Big Yellow Dog Music, 2001/Tokeco Tunes, 2001/Tree Publishing, 2001
Performed by Toby Keith on the album *Pull My Chain* (DreamWorks, 2001).

I'm Like a Bird
Words and music by Nelly Furtado
Nelstar Publishing, 2000
Performed by Nelly Furtado on the album *Whoa, Nelly!* (DreamWorks, 2000). Won a Grammy Award for Best Female Pop Vocal Performance, 2001. Nominated for a Grammy Award, Song of the Year, 2001.

I'm Real
Words and music by Martin Denny, Leshaun Lewis, Jennifer Lopez, Troy Oliver, and Cory Rooney
Cori Tiffani Publishing, 2001/Nuyorican Publishing, 2001/Sony ATV Songs LLC, 2001/Chocolate Factory Music, 2001/Alpha Music, 2001
Performed by Jennifer Lopez featuring Ja Rule on the album *J.Lo* (Epic, 2001). Also featured on the Ja Rule album *Pain Is Love* (Def Jam, 2001).

I'm a Slave 4 U
Words and music by Charles Hugo and Pharrell Williams
Chase Chad Music, 2001/EMI-April Music, 2001/EMI-Blackwood Music Inc., 2001/Waters of Nazareth Publishing, 2001
Performed by Britney Spears on the album *Britney* (Jive, 2001).

I'm a Survivor
Words and music by Shelby Kennedy and Phillip White
Murrah Music, 2001/Porch Pickin' Publishing, 2001
Performed by Reba McEntire on the album *Greatest Hits, Volume III: I'm a Survivor* (MCA Nashville, 2001).

I'm a Thug
Words and music by Trick Daddy (pseudonym for Maurice Young),

Adam Duggins, and Rafe Van Hoy
First and Gold Publishing, 2001/Tree Publishing, 2001
Performed by Trick Daddy on the album *Thugs Are Us* (Atlantic, 2001).

I'm Tryin'

Words and music by Chris Wallin, Jeffrey Steele, and Anthony Smith
4T4 Music, 2001/Almo Music Corp., 2001/Gottahaveable Music, 2001/
    Songs of Windswept Pacific, 2001/Pacific Wind Music, 2001
Performed by Trace Adkins on the album *Chrome* (Capitol Nashville,
    2001).

Imitation of Life

Words and music by Peter Buck, Michael Mills, and Michael Stipe
Temporary Music, 2001
Performed by R.E.M. on the album *Reveal* (Warner Bros., 2001).
    Nominated for a Grammy Award, Best Pop Performance by a Duo or
    Group With Vocal, 2001.

In California

Words and music by Michael Flanagan, Lisa Marr, David Philips, and
    Sherri Solinger
Silent Movies for the Blind, 2001
Performed by Neko Case on the album *Canadian Amp* (Lady Pilot,
    2001).

In the End

Words and music by Chester Bennington, Rob Bourdon, Brad Delson,
    Joseph Hahn, and Mike Shinoda
Zomba Enterprises, 2000/Chesterchaz Publishing, 2000/Zomba Songs,
    2000/Nondisclosure Agreement Music, 2000/Rob Bourdon Music,
    2000/Kenji Kobayashi Music, 2000
Performed by Linkin Park on the album *Hybrid Theory* (Warner Bros.,
    2000).

In the Jailhouse Now

Words and music by Jimmie Rodgers
APRS Music, 1962
Covered by the fictional band the Soggy Bottom Boys (Dan Tyminski,
    Harley Allen, Pat Enright) featuring Tim Blake Nelson on the movie
    soundtrack album *O Brother, Where Art Thou?* (Lost Highway, 2000).
    Originally performed by Jimmie Rodgers.

In My Secret Life

Words by Leonard Cohen, music by Sharon Robinson
Sharon Robinson Songs, 2001/Sony ATV Songs LLC, 2001
Performed by Leonard Cohen on the album *Ten New Songs* (Columbia,
    2001).

Innocent
Words and music by Carl Bell
Pener Pig Publishing, 2000/Universal Songs of Polygram Intntl., 2000
Performed by Fuel on the album *Something Like Human* (Epic/550, 2000).

Inside Out
Words and music by Bryan Adams and Gretchen Peters
Badams Music Ltd., Dublin 2, Ireland, 1998/Purple Crayon Music, 1998/Sony ATV Tunes LLC, 1998
Covered by Trisha Yearwood featuring Don Henley on the album *Inside Out* (MCA Nashville, 2001). Originally performed by Bryan Adams on the album *On a Day Like Today* (A&M, 1998). Nominated for a Grammy Award, Best Country Collaboration With Vocals, 2001.

Irresistible
Words and music by Anders Bagge, Arnthor Birgisson, and Pamela Sheyne
EMI-Blackwood Music Inc., 2001/Murlyn Songs, 2001/Warner-Tamerlane Publishing, 2001/Plum Tree Tunes, 2001/Air Chrysalis Scandinavia, 2001/Universal Polygram International Pub., 2001
Performed by Jessica Simpson on the album *Irresistible* (Columbia, 2001).

Is That Your Chick (The Lost Verses)
Words and music by Memphis Bleek (pseudonym for Malik Cox), Missy Elliott, Jay-Z (pseudonym for Shawn Carter), Carl Mitchell, and Timbaland (pseudonym for Timothy Mosley)
EMI-Blackwood Music Inc., 2000/Lil Lu Lu Publishing, 2000/Virginia Beach Music, 2000/Mass Confusion Productions, 2000/Sticky Green, 2000
Performed by Memphis Bleek featuring Jay-Z, Twista, and Missy Elliott on the album *The Understanding* (Def Jam, 2000).

Is This It
Words and music by Julian Casablancas
The Strokes Band Music, 2001
Performed by the Strokes on the album *Is This It* (RCA, 2001).

Island in the Sun
Words and music by Rivers Cuomo
E. O. Smith Music, 2001
Performed by Weezer on the album *Weezer* (Geffen, 2001).

It Began in Afrika
Music by Tom Rowlands, Ed Simons, and James Ingram
Universal-MCA Music Publishing, 2001/Copyright Control, 2001

Performed by the Chemical Brothers. Released as a single (Astralwerks, 2001).

It Wasn't Me
Words by Shaggy (pseudonym for Orville Burrell) and Ricardo Ducent, words and music by Shaun Pizzonia
Livingsting Music, 2000
Performed by Shaggy featuring Ricardo "RikRok" Ducent on the album *Hotshot* (MCA, 2000). Nominated for a Grammy Award, Best Pop Collaboration With Vocals, 2001.

The Itch
Words and music by Vitamin C (pseudonym for Colleen Fitzpatrick), Billy Steinberg, and Jimmy Harry
Jerk Awake Music, Los Angeles, 2000/Blanc E Music, 2000/Warner-Tamerlane Publishing, 2000/EMI-Virgin Music, 2000/Whorga Music, 2000
Performed by Vitamin C on the album *More* (Elektra, 2000).

It's Been Awhile
Words and music by John April, Aaron Lewis, Michael Mushok, and Jonathan Wysocki
Greenfund, 2000/I'm Nobody Music, 2000/My Blue Car Music, 2000/Pimp Yug, 2000/WB Music Publishing, 2000
Performed by Staind on the album *Break the Cycle* (Flip/Elektra, 2001).

It's a Great Day to Be Alive
Words and music by Darrell Scott
EMI-April Music, 1997/House of Bram, 1997
Covered by Travis Tritt on the album *Down the Road I Go* (Columbia, 2000). Originally performed by Darrell Scott on the album *Aloha From Nashville* (Sugar Hill, 1997).

It's Over
Words and music by Roman Coppola, Christopher Davis, Jermaine Dupri, La Marquis Jefferson, and Run (pseudonym for Joseph Simmons)
Bug Music, 2001/EMI-Blackwood Music Inc., 2001/Ground Control Music, 2001/King Swing Music, 2001/Carmit Music, 2001/EMI-April Music, 2001/Protoons Inc., 2001/So So Def Music, 2001
Performed by Run-D.M.C. featuring Jermaine Dupri on the album *Crown Royal* (Arista, 2001).

It's Over Now
Words and music by Melvin Glover, Daron Jones, Michael Keith, Quinnes Parker, Sylvia Robinson, and Marvin Scandrick
Da 12 Music, 2001/EMI-April Music, 2001/Justin Combs Publishing, 2001/Liquid Liquid Publishing, 2001/Sugar Hill Music Publishing,

Ltd., 2001/Twenty Nine Black Music, 2001
Performed by 112 on the album *Part III* (Bad Boy, 2001).

Izzo (H.O.V.A.)
Words and music by Jay-Z (pseudonym for Shawn Carter), Alphonso
   Mizell, Frederick Perren, Deke Richards, and Kanye West, music by
   Berry Gordy
EMI-Blackwood Music Inc., 2001/Lil Lu Lu Publishing, 2001/Jobete
   Music Co., 2001
Performed by Jay-Z on the album *The Blueprint* (Def Jam, 2001).
   Nominated for a Grammy Award, Best Rap Solo Performance, 2001.

J

Jacksonville Skyline
Words and music by Ryan Adams
Barland Music, 2001
Performed by Whiskeytown on the album *Pneumonia* (Lost Highway, 2001).

Jaded
Words and music by Steven Tyler (pseudonym for Steven Tallarico) and Martin Frederiksen
Demon of Screamin Music, 2001/EMI-April Music, 2001/EMI-Blackwood Music Inc., 2001/Pearl White Music, 2001
Performed by Aerosmith on the album *Just Push Play* (Columbia, 2001). Nominated for Grammy Awards, Best Rock Performance by a Duo or Group With Vocal, 2001, and Best Rock Song, 2001.

Jumpin' & Bumpin'
Words and music by Zack Toms and Paul Simpson
Paul Simpson Music, 1998
Performed by Kim English. Released as a single (Nervous, 2001).

Just in Case
Words and music by Edward Berkeley, Keir Gist, and Robert Huggar
Divine Mill Music, 2001/EMI-April Music, 2001/Fingaz Goal Music, 2001/Uh Oh Entertainment, 2001
Performed by Jaheim on the album *Ghetto Love* (Warner Bros., 2001).

Just Friends (Sunny)
Words and music by Musiq Soulchild (pseudonym for Taalib Johnson), Carvin Haggins, and Robert Hebb
Notable Music Co., 2000/Portable Music Company, 2000
Performed by Musiq Soulchild on the movie soundtrack album *Nutty Professor II: The Klumps* (Def Jam, 2000). Later featured on the Musiq Soulchild album *Aijuswanaseing* (Def Jam, 2000).

Just Keep Thinking About You
Words and music by Gwendolyn Cathey and Harold Johnson
Jobete Music Co., 2001
Performed by Gloria Gaynor. Released as a single (Logic, 2001).

Just Push Play
Words and music by Stephen Dudas, Mark Hudson, and Steven Tyler
  (pseudonym for Steven Tallarico)
Beef Puppet Music, 2001/Demon of Screamin Music, 2001/EMI-April
  Music, 2001/S'More Music, 2001/Universal-MCA Music Publishing,
  2001
Performed by Aerosmith on the album *Just Push Play* (Columbia,
  2001).

K

Keep Control
Words and music by Florian Sikorski and Martin Weiland
Warner-Tamerlane Publishing, 2001
Performed by Sono. Released as a single (Strictly Rhythm, 2001).

King of El Paso
Words and music by Boz Scaggs and Jack Walroth
Jack Walroth Music, 2001/Windover Lake Songs, 2001
Performed by Boz Scaggs on the album *Dig* (Virgin, 2001).

Knives Out
Words and music by Colin Greenwood, Jonathan Greenwood, Edward
  O'Brien, Philip Selway, and Thomas Yorke
Warner-Chappell Music, 2001
Performed by Radiohead on the album *Amnesiac* (Capitol, 2001).

L

La Bomba
Words and music by Fabio Zambrana
Sony/ATV Discos Music Publishing, 1998
Performed by Azul Azul on the album *El Sapo* (Sony Discos, 2000).

La Cienega Just Smiled
Words and music by Ryan Adams
Barland Music, 2001
Performed by Ryan Adams on the album *Gold* (Lost Highway, 2001).

La La Land
Words and music by Charlotte Caffey and Kathryn Valentine
Chargo Music, 2001
Performed by the Go-Go's on the album *God Bless the Go-Go's*
  (Beyond, 2001).

Lady (Hear Me Tonight)
Words and music by Yann Destagnol and Romain Tranchart
Universal Musica, 2000
Performed by Modjo. Initially released as a single (MCA, 2000); later
  featured on the album *Modjo* (MCA, 2001).

Lady Marmalade
Words and music by Bob Crewe and Kenny Nolan
Jobete Music Co., 1974/Kenny Nolan Publishing, 1974/Stone Diamond
  Music, 1974/Tannyboy Music, 1974
Covered by Christina Aguilera, Lil' Kim, Mya, and Pink on the movie
  soundtrack album *Moulin Rouge* (Interscope, 2001). Originally
  performed by LaBelle. Won a Grammy Award for Best Pop
  Collaboration With Vocals, 2001.

Laredo
Words and music by Christopher Cagle
Mark Hybner Publishing, 2000

Performed by Chris Cagle on the album *Play It Loud* (Virgin Nashville, 2000).

Last Flight Out
Words and music by Alexandra Talomaa
Zomba Enterprises, 2000
Performed by Plus One on the album *The Promise* (Atlantic, 2000).

Last Good Day of the Year
Words and music by Davey Ray Moor
Rykomusic, 2001/Pubco Music, 2001
Performed by Cousteau on the album *Cousteau* (Palm Pictures, 2000).

Last Night a DJ Saved My Life
Words and music by Michael Cleveland
Comart Music, 1982/EMI Longitude Music, 1982
Covered by Mariah Carey featuring Busta Rhymes, Fabolous, and DJ
  Clue on the movie soundtrack album *Glitter* (Virgin, 2001).
  Originally performed by Indeep.

Last Nite
Words and music by Julian Casablancas
The Strokes Band Music, 2001
Performed by the Strokes on the album *Is This It* (RCA, 2001).

Lay Low
Words and music by Snoop Dogg (pseudonym for Calvin Broadus),
  Tracey Davis, Michael Elizondo, Nate Dogg (pseudonym for
  Nathaniel Hale), Danny Means, Master P (pseudonym for Percy
  Miller), Keiwan Spillman, and Dr. Dre (pseudonym for Andre Young)
Ain't Nothing but Funkin', 2001/Blotter Music, 2001/Elvis Mambo
  Music, 2001/Means Family Publishing, 2001/Music of Windswept,
  2001/Tray Tray's Music, 2001/Big P Music, 2001/Brea and Nea
  Music, 2001/My Own Chit Publishing, 2001/Nate Dogg Music, 2001
Performed by Snoop Dogg featuring Nate Dogg and Master P on the
  album *Tha Last Meal* (No Limit/Priority, 2000).

Leave It Up to Me
Words and music by Michael Power and Lucas Secon
Zomba Enterprises, 2001/Warner-Tamerlane Publishing, 2001/Zomba
  Management Publ. Ltd., 2001
Performed by Aaron Carter on the movie soundtrack album *Jimmy
  Neutron: Boy Genius* (Jive, 2001).

Left Behind
Words and music by Michael Crahan, Christopher Fehn, Paul Gray,
  Craig Jones, Nathan Jordison, James Root, Corey Taylor, Nicholas
  Thompson, and Sidney Wilson
EMI-April Music, 2001/Music That Music, 2001

Performed by Slipknot on the album *Iowa* (Roadrunner, 2001).
Nominated for a Grammy Award, Best Metal Performance, 2001.

Let Me Blow Ya Mind
Words and music by Eve (pseudonym for Eve Jeffers), Michael
Elizondo, and Dr. Dre (pseudonym for Andre Young), music by Scott
Storch
Ain't Nothing but Funkin', 2001/Blondie Rockwell Music, 2001/Blotter
Music, 2001/Elvis Mambo Music, 2001/TVT Music, 2001/Universal-
MCA Music Publishing, 2001/WB Music Publishing, 2001
Performed by Eve featuring Gwen Stefani on the album *Scorpion*
(Interscope, 2001). Won a Grammy Award for Best Rap/Sung
Collaboration, 2001.

Let's Roll
Words and music by Neil Young
Silver Fiddle Music, 2001
Performed by Neil Young. Inspired by the actions of United Airlines
Flight 93 passengers during the September 11th, 2001, terrorist
attacks. Released as a single (Reprise, 2001).

Life on a Chain
Words and music by Peter Yorn
Boyletown Music, 2001
Performed by Pete Yorn on the album *Musicforthemorningafter*
(Columbia, 2001).

Lifetime
Words and music by Hod David and Maxwell
Famous Music Corp., 2001/Gan Zmira, 2001/Muszewell Music, 2001
Performed by Maxwell on the album *Now* (Columbia, 2001). Nominated
for a Grammy Award, Best Male R&B Vocal Performance, 2001.

Like Wow!
Words and music by James Harry and Sandra St. Victor
EMI-Virgin Music, 2001/Maanami Music, 2001/Whorga Music, 2001
Performed by Leslie Carter. Released as a single (DreamWorks, 2001).

Little L
Words and music by Jason Kay and Toby Smith
EMI-Blackwood Music Inc., 2001/EMI Music Publishing Ltd., 2001
Performed by Jamiroquai on the album *A Funk Odyssey* (Epic, 2001).

Little Sparrow
Words and music by Dolly Parton
Velvet Apple Music, 2000
Performed by Dolly Parton on the album *Little Sparrow* (Sugar Hill,
2001).

Livin' It Up
Words and music by Ja Rule (pseudonym for Jeffrey Atkins), Irv Gotti
(pseudonym for Irving Lorenzo), and Robin Mays, music by Stevie
Wonder
Black Bull Music, 2001/Jobete Music Co., 2001/DJ Irv Publishing,
2001/Ensign Music, 2001/Slavery Music, 2001/Songs of Universal,
2001
Performed by Ja Rule featuring Case on the album *Pain Is Love* (Def
Jam, 2001). Nominated for a Grammy Award, Best Rap/Sung
Collaboration, 2001.

Livin' for Love
Words and music by Natalie Cole, Denise Rich, and Garianno Lorenzo
Connotation Music, 2000/Cole-Arama Music, 2000/Dream Image IDG
Publishing, 2000/Garianno Music Publishing, 2000/Music on the Net,
2000
Performed by Natalie Cole on the album *Greatest Hits, Volume I*
(Elektra, 2000).

Lonely Girls
Words and music by Lucinda Williams
Lucy Jones Music, 2001/Warner-Tamerlane Publishing, 2001
Performed by Lucinda Williams on the album *Essence* (Lost Highway,
2001).

Long Gone Lonesome Blues
Words and music by Hank Williams
Acuff Rose Music, 1950/Rightsong Music, 1950
Covered by Sheryl Crow on the tribute album *Hank Williams: Timeless*
(Lost Highway, 2001). Originally performed by Hank Williams.
Nominated for a Grammy Award, Best Female Country Vocal
Performance, 2001.

A Long Walk
Words and music by Andre Harris and Jill Scott
Blue's Baby Music, 2000/Dirty Dre Music, 2000
Performed by Jill Scott on the album *Who Is Jill Scott? Words and
Sounds, Vol. 1* (Hidden Beach/Epic, 2000). Nominated for a Grammy
Award, Best Female R&B Vocal Performance, 2001.

Look at Us
Words and music by Carlo Marchino and Sarina Paris
EMI-Blackwood Music Inc., 2000/EMI Music Publishing Italia, 2000
Performed by Sarina Paris. Initially released as a single (Priority, 2000);
later featured on the album *Sarina Paris* (Priority, 2001).

Love
Words and music by Musiq Soulchild (pseudonym for Taalib Johnson),

Andre Harris, and Carvin Haggins

Dirty Dre Music, 2001/EMI-April Music, 2001/Nivrac Tyke Music, 2001/Soul Child Music, 2001/Touched by Jazz Music, 2001

Performed by Musiq Soulchild on the album *Aijuswanaseing* (Def Jam, 2000). Nominated for a Grammy Award, Best Male R&B Vocal Performance, 2001.

A Love Before Time

Words and music by Jorge Calandrelli and James Schamus, music by Tan Dun

Parnassus Productions, 2000/Sony ATV Tunes LLC, 2000

Performed by CoCo Lee on the movie soundtrack album *Crouching Tiger, Hidden Dragon* (Sony Classical, 2000). Nominated for a Grammy Award, Best Song Written for a Motion Picture/Television, 2001.

Love Don't Cost a Thing

Words and music by Georgette Franklin, Amille Harris, Greg Lawson, Jeremy Monroe, and Damon Sharpe

Connotation Music, 2001/Reach Global Songs, 2001/Warner-Tamerlane Publishing, 2001/J-Rated Music, 2001/Swette Ya' Music, 2001/Damon Sharpe Music, 2001/Annotation Music, 2001/GQ Romeo Music, 2001/God's Child Music, 2001

Performed by Jennifer Lopez on the album *J.Lo* (Epic, 2001).

Love Is Enough

Words and music by Joe Thrasher and James Varsos

Willdawn Music, 2000/Rio Bravo Music, 2000

Performed by 3 of Hearts on the album *3 of Hearts* (RCA, 2001).

Love Letters

Words by Edward Heyman, music by Victor Young

Famous Music Corp., 1945

Covered by Diana Krall on the album *The Look of Love* (Verve, 2001). Originally performed by Dick Haymes.

Love Letters From Old Mexico

Words and music by Leslie Satcher

Ensign Music, 2000

Performed by Leslie Satcher on the album *Love Letters* (Warner Bros. Nashville, 2000).

Love of My Life

Words and music by Brian McKnight

Universal Polygram International Pub., 2001

Performed by Brian McKnight on the album *Superhero* (Motown, 2001). Nominated for Grammy Awards, Best Male R&B Vocal Performance, 2001, and Best R&B Song, 2001.

Love of a Woman
Words and music by Kevin Hildebrandt
Songs of Lastrada, 2000
Performed by Travis Tritt on the album *Down the Road I Go*
  (Columbia, 2000).

Loverboy
Words and music by Mariah Carey, Thomas Jenkins, and Larry
  Blackmon
Better Half Music Co., 2001/Fox Film Music Corp., 2001/Rye Songs,
  2001/Sony ATV Songs LLC, 2001/Universal Songs of Polygram
  Intntl., 2001/All Seeing Eye, 2001
Performed by Mariah Carey featuring Cameo on the movie soundtrack
  album *Glitter* (Virgin, 2001).

Lovesick Blues
Words and music by Cliff Friend and Irving Mills
EMI Mills Music, 1949
Covered by Ryan Adams on the tribute album *Hank Williams: Timeless*
  (Lost Highway, 2001). Originally performed by Hank Williams.
  Nominated for a Grammy Award, Best Male Country Vocal
  Performance, 2001.

Lovin' You
Words and music by Kristine W (pseudonym for Kristine Weitz), Maria
  Christensen, Karsten Dahlgaard, Vince Degiorgio, and Johnny
  Pedersen
Careers-BMG Music, 2000/BMG Music Publishing Canada, 2000/C2 It
  Music Publishing, 2000/Sweet Woo Music, 2000/Denotation Music,
  2000/Champion Music Ltd., 2000/Weitz House Publishing, 2000
Performed by Kristine W on the album *Stronger* (RCA, 2000).

Lucky 4 You (Tonight I'm Just Me)
Words and music by Jason Deere, Lisa Hamilton-Brown, and Kristyn
  Osborn
Lehsem Music LLC, 1999/Scott Hendricks Corporation, 1999/WB
  Music Publishing, 1999/Without Anna Music, 1999
Performed by SHeDAISY on the album *The Whole Shebang* (Lyric
  Street, 1999).

The Lucky One
Words and music by Robert Lee Castleman
Live Slow Music, 2001
Performed by Alison Krauss & Union Station on the album *New
  Favorite* (Rounder, 2001). Won Grammy Awards.

M

Mad Season
Words and music by Robert Thomas
Bidnis Inc., 2000/EMI-Blackwood Music Inc., 2000
Performed by Matchbox Twenty on the album *Mad Season* (Lava/
   Atlantic, 2000).

Mamacita
Words and music by Gromyko Collins and Travon Potts
Dreamworks Songs, 2000/Nakita's Publishing, 2000/Travon Music,
   2000/Universal Polygram International Pub., 2000
Performed by Public Announcement on the album *Don't Hold Back*
   (RCA, 2001).

Marie
Words and music by Townes Van Zandt
Townes Van Zandt Music, 1989
Performed by Willie Nelson on the album *Poet: A Tribute to Townes
   Van Zandt* (Freefalls Entertainment, 2001). Originally performed by
   Townes Van Zandt. Nominated for a Grammy Award, Best Male
   Country Vocal Performance, 2001.

May It Be
Words by Roma Ryan, music by Enya (pseudonym for Eithne Ni
   Bhraonain) and Nicky Ryan
EMI-Blackwood Music Inc., 2000
Performed by Enya in the movie and on the soundtrack album *The Lord
   of the Rings: The Fellowship of the Ring* (Reprise, 2001). Nominated
   for an Academy Award, Best Original Song, 2001.

Maybe I Deserve
Words and music by Tank (pseudonym for Durrell Babbs)
Black Fountain Music, 2001
Performed by Tank on the album *Force of Nature* (Blackground, 2001).

Midwest Swing

Words and music by Nelly (pseudonym for Cornell Haynes), Jason Epperson, Robert Cleveland, Tohri Harper, and Ali Jones

Jay E's Basement, 2001/Universal-MCA Music Publishing, 2001/BMG Songs Inc., 2001/Jackie Frost Music, 2001/Sam Swap Publishing, 2001/D2 Pro Publishing, 2001/Young Dude Publishing, 2001/Da Bess Publishing, 2001

Performed by St. Lunatics on the album *Free City* (Universal, 2001).

Missing You

Words and music by Tim Kelley, Bob Robinson, Joe Thomas, and Joshua Thompson

563 Music Publishing, 2001/Tallest Tree Music, 2001/Zomba Enterprises, 2001/Cherry River Music, 2001/Time for Flytes Music, 2001

Performed by Case on the album *Open Letter* (Def Jam, 2001). Nominated for a Grammy Award, Best Male R&B Vocal Performance, 2001.

Mississippi

Words and music by Bob Dylan (pseudonym for Robert Zimmerman)

Special Rider Music, 1997

Performed by Bob Dylan on the album *Love and Theft* (Columbia, 2001). Originally performed by Sheryl Crow on the album *The Globe Sessions* (A&M, 1998).

The Modern Age

Words and music by Julian Casablancas

The Strokes Band Music, 2001

Performed by the Strokes on the album *Is This It* (RCA, 2001).

More Than That

Words and music by Adam Anders, Fredrik Jernberg, and Pontus Wennerberg

Sony ATV Tunes LLC, 2001/Universal Polygram International Pub., 2001/Sony ATV Songs LLC, 2001

Performed by the Backstreet Boys on the album *Black & Blue* (Jive, 2000).

Mrs. Steven Rudy

Words and music by Shane Decker and Mark McGuinn

Cal IV Entertainment Inc., 2001/Neon Mule Music Publishing, 2001/WB Music Publishing, 2001

Performed by Mark McGuinn on the album *Mark McGuinn* (VFR, 2001).

Ms. Jackson

Words and music by Andre Benjamin, David Sheats, and Antwan Patton

Dungeon Rat Music, 2000/Chrysalis Music, 2000/Gnat Booty Music, 2000/EMI-April Music, 2000
Performed by Outkast on the album *Stankonia* (LaFace/Arista, 2000). Won a Grammy Award for Best Rap Performance by a Duo or Group, 2001. Nominated for Grammy Awards, Best Short Form Music Video, 2001, and Record of the Year, 2001.

Munster Rag
Music by Brad Paisley, James Gregory, and Mitch McMichen
EMI-April Music, 2001/Sea Gayle Music, 2001/Music Alley, 2001/ Trudysong Music, 2000
Performed by Brad Paisley on the album *Part II* (Arista Nashville, 2001). Nominated for a Grammy Award, Best Country Instrumental Performance, 2001.

Music
Words and music by Erick Sermon and Marvin Gaye
EMI-April Music, 2001/Erick Sermon Enterprises, 2001
Performed by Erick Sermon featuring Marvin Gaye on the album *Music* (J Records, 2001).

My Baby
Words and music by Berry Gordy, Alphonso Mizell, Frederick Perren, and Deke Richards
Jobete Music Co., 2001
Performed by Lil' Romeo on the album *Lil' Romeo* (Soulja Music Entertainment/Priority, 2001).

My Baby You
Words and music by Walter Afanasieff and Marc Anthony
Sony Tunes, 1999
Performed by Marc Anthony on the album *Marc Anthony* (Columbia, 1999).

My Cellmate Thinks I'm Sexy
Words by Cledus T. Judd (pseudonym for Barry Poole) and Chris Clark, music by Jim Collins and Paul Overstreet
EMI-Blackwood Music Inc., 1999/Jelinda Music, 1999/Scarlet Moon Music, 1999
Performed by Cledus T. Judd on the album *Just Another Day in Parodies* (Monument, 2000). Based on the Kenny Chesney song "She Thinks My Tractor's Sexy."

My Everything
Words and music by Anders Bagge, Arnthor Birgisson, Nick Lachey, and Justin Jeffre
98 Degrees and Rising, 2000/Chrysalis Music, 2000/EMI-April Music,

2000/Universal Polygram International Pub., 2000
Performed by 98 Degrees on the album *Revelation* (Universal, 2000).

My First Love
Words and music by Ivan Moore and Angela Winbush
Angel Notes Music, 1983/Suti Music, 1983
Covered by Avant featuring Ketara Wyatt on the album *My Thoughts*
(Magic Johnson Music, 2000). Originally performed by Rene and
Angela.

My Funny Friend and Me
Words and music by David Hartley and Sting (pseudonym for Gordon
Sumner)
Wonderland Music, 2000
Performed by Sting on the movie soundtrack album *The Emperor's New
Groove* (Disney, 2000). Nominated for a Grammy Award, Best Song
Written for a Motion Picture/Television, 2001.

My Kind of Girl
Words and music by Brian McKnight
Universal Polygram International Pub., 2001
Performed by Brian McKnight featuring Justin Timberlake on the album
Superhero (Motown, 2001). Nominated for a Grammy Award, Best
Pop Collaboration With Vocals, 2001.

My Love Goes On and On
Words and music by Christopher Cagle and Don Pfrimmer
Cross Keys Publishing, 1997/Platinum Plow, 1997/WB Music
Publishing, 1997
Performed by Chris Cagle on the album *Play It Loud* (Virgin Nashville,
2000).

My Projects
Words and music by Coo Coo Cal (pseudonym for Calvin Bellamy),
music by Henry Cook
From the Pit Publishing, 2001
Performed by Coo Coo Cal on the album *Disturbed* (Tommy Boy,
2001).

My Sacrifice
Words and music by Scott Stapp and Mark Tremonti
Dwight Frye Music, 2001/Tremonti Stapp Music, 2001
Performed by Creed on the album *Weathered* (Wind-Up, 2001).

My Way
Words by Frederick Durst, music by Eric Barrier, Wesley Borland, Leor
Dimant, William Griffin, John Otto, and Samuel Rivers
Big Bizkit Music, 2000/Zomba Enterprises, 2000

Performed by Limp Bizkit on the album *Chocolate St*rfish and the Hot Dog Flavored Water* (Interscope, 2000).

N

Naive Song
Music by Mirwais (pseudonym for Mirwais Ahmadzai)
Warner-Tamerlane Publishing, 2000/Copyright Control, 2000
Performed by Mirwais on the album *Production* (Epic, 2000).

Neighborhoods
Words and music by Olu Dara (pseudonym for Charles Jones)
Odar Publishing, 2001/WB Music Publishing, 2001
Performed by Olu Dara on the album *Neighborhoods* (Atlantic, 2001).

Never Be the Same Again
Words and music by Ghostface Killah (pseudonym for Dennis Coles),
  Davel McKenzie, Sergio Moore, Brian Palmer, and Raekwon
  (pseudonym for Corey Woods)
Carpa Noche, 2001/Davel McKenzie Publishing, 2001/Starks Publishing,
  2001/Warner-Tamerlane Publishing, 2001/In Tha Blood Music, 2001/
  Careers-BMG Music, 2001/Wu-Tang Publishing, 2001
Performed by Ghostface Killah featuring Carl Thomas and Raekwon on
  the album *Bulletproof Wallets* (Epic, 2001).

Never Had a Dream Come True
Words and music by Catherine Dennis and Simon Ellis
BMG Songs Inc., 2000/Colgems-EMI Music, 2000
Performed by S Club 7 on the album *7* (Interscope, 2001).

Never Too Far
Words and music by Mariah Carey, James Harris, III, and Terry Lewis
Fox Film Music Corp., 2001/Rye Songs, 2001/Sony ATV Songs LLC,
  2001/EMI-April Music, 2001/Flyte Tyme Tunes, 2001
Performed by Mariah Carey on the movie soundtrack album *Glitter*
  (Virgin, 2001).

New York City Cops
Words and music by Julian Casablancas
The Strokes Band Music, 2001

Performed by the Strokes on the album *Is This It* (RCA, 2001).
 Removed from U.S. edition of album following the terrorist attacks of
 September 11th, 2001.

New York, New York
Words and music by Ryan Adams
Barland Music, 2001
Performed by Ryan Adams on the album *Gold* (Lost Highway, 2001).
 Nominated for a Grammy Award, Best Male Rock Vocal
 Performance, 2001.

New York State of Mind
Words and music by Billy Joel
Joelsongs, 1975
Covered by Tony Bennett featuring Billy Joel on the album *Playin'
 With My Friends: Bennett Sings the Blues* (Columbia, 2001).
 Originally performed by Billy Joel on the album *Turnstiles*
 (Columbia, 1976). Nominated for a Grammy Award, Best Pop
 Collaboration With Vocals, 2001.

Nico
Words and music by Ian Astbury and Billy Duffy
Tayminster Ltd., 2001/Screenchoice Ltd., 2001
Performed by the Cult on the album *Beyond Good and Evil* (Lava/
 Atlantic, 2001).

No More (Baby I'ma Do Right)
Words and music by Nathan Butler, Cameron Giles, and Sean Hall
Faith Force, 2000/Famous Music Corp., 2000/Gimme Some Hot Sauce
 Music, 2000/Tunes on the Verge of Insanity, 2000/Zomba Enterprises,
 2000/Killa Cam Music, 2000/Un Rivera Publishing, 2000/Warner-
 Tamerlane Publishing, 2000
Performed by 3LW on the album *3LW* (Epic, 2000).

No More Drama
Words and music by James Harris, III and Terry Lewis, music by Perry
 Botkin, Jr. and Barry de Vorzon
Screen Gems-EMI Music Inc., 2001/EMI-April Music, 2001/Flyte Tyme
 Tunes, 2001
Performed by Mary J. Blige on the album *No More Drama* (MCA,
 2001).

Nobody Wants to Be Lonely
Words and music by Desmond Child, Gary Burr, and Victoria Shaw
Deston Songs, 2000/Universal-MCA Music Publishing, 2000/Victoria
 Shaw Songs, 2000/Gabburr Tunes, 2000/Desmundo Music, 2000
Performed by Ricky Martin featuring Christina Aguilera on the album

Sound Loaded (Columbia, 2000). Nominated for a Grammy Award, Best Pop Collaboration With Vocals, 2001.

None Tonight
Words and music by Lil' Zane (pseudonym for Zane Copeland), Dyonna Lewis, and Ricciano Lumpkins
Soundtron Tunes, 2000/Tycon Music, 2000/Platinum World Publishing, 2000/Dole's Mix Music, 2000/Kalinmia Music, 2000/Lil' Nettie Music, 2000
Performed by Lil' Zane on the album *Young World: The Future* (Priority, 2000).

O

O Death
Traditional
Performed by Ralph Stanley in the movie and on the soundtrack album
  O Brother, Where Art Thou? (Lost Highway, 2000). Won a Grammy
  Award for Best Male Country Vocal Performance, 2001.

Oh No
Words and music by Nate Dogg (pseudonym for Nathaniel Hale), Troy
  Jamerson, Mos Def (pseudonym for Dante Smith), and Dana Stinson
Warner-Chappell Music, 2000/EMI-Blackwood Music Inc., 2000/Empire
  International Music, 2000/Medina Sounds Music, 2000/Nate Dogg
  Music, 2000/Trescadecaphobia Music, 2000/Warner-Tamerlane
  Publishing, 2000
Performed by Mos Def, Pharoahe Monch, and Nate Dogg on the
  various-artists album *Lyricist Lounge 2* (Rawkus, 2000).

Oklahoma
Words and music by John Allen and David Williams
Simranch Songs, 2000/Songs of Alexhan, 2000/Thanks To Van
  Publishing, 2000/WB Music Publishing, 2000
Performed by Billy Gilman on the album *One Voice* (Epic, 2000).

On the Line
Words and music by Steven Diamond, Mark Hammond, and Samuel
  Vann
Hand Picked Songs, 2001/Mark Hammond Music, 2001/Real Diamonds,
  2001
Performed by the On the Line All-Stars (Lance Bass, Joey Fatone,
  Mandy Moore, Christian Burns, True Vibe) on the movie soundtrack
  album *On the Line* (Jive, 2001).

On a Night Like This
Words and music by Doug Kahan and Karen Staley
Instinct Music, 2001/Warner-Tamerlane Publishing, 2001

Performed by Trick Pony on the album *Trick Pony* (Warner Bros., 2001).

One Minute Man
Words and music by Missy Elliott, Ludacris (pseudonym for Christopher Bridges), Timbaland (pseudonym for Timothy Mosley), and David Pomeranz
EMI-April Music, 2001/Ludacris Music Publishing, 2001/Mass Confusion Productions, 2001/Virginia Beach Music, 2001/WB Music Publishing, 2001
Performed by Missy Elliott featuring Ludacris on the album *Miss E . . . So Addictive* (The Gold Mind/Elektra, 2001). Nominated for a Grammy Award, Best Short Form Music Video, 2001.

One More Day
Words and music by Steven Jones and Bobby Tomberlin
Mike Curb Music, 2000/Sound Island Music, 2000/EMI-April Music, 2000
Performed by Diamond Rio on the album *One More Day* (Arista Nashville, 2001). Nominated for Grammy Awards, Best Country Performance by a Duo/Group With Vocal, 2001, and Best Country Song, 2001.

One More Time
Words and music by Thomas Bangalter, Guy de Homem-Christo, and Anthony Moore
Reach Global Songs, 2000/Ttuff Ttony Music, 2000/Zomba Songs, 2000
Performed by Daft Punk featuring Romanthony on the album *Discovery* (Virgin, 2001). Nominated for a Grammy Award, Best Dance Recording, 2001.

One Step Closer
Words and music by Chester Bennington, Rob Bourdon, Brad Delson, Joseph Hahn, and Mike Shinoda
Zomba Enterprises, 2000/Chesterchaz Publishing, 2000/Zomba Songs, 2000/Nondisclosure Agreement Music, 2000/Rob Bourdon Music, 2000/Kenji Kobayashi Music, 2000
Performed by Linkin Park on the album *Hybrid Theory* (Warner Bros., 2000). Also featured on the movie soundtrack album *Dracula 2000* (Sony, 2000).

One Woman Man
Words and music by Mike City (pseudonym for Michael Flowers)
Mike City Music, 2000/Warner-Tamerlane Publishing, 2000
Performed by Dave Hollister on the album *Chicago '85 . . . the Movie* (DreamWorks, 2000).

Only in America
Words and music by Kix Brooks (pseudonym for Leon Brooks, III), Don Cook, and Ronnie Rogers
Buffalo Prairie Songs, 2001/Don Cook Music, 2001/Route Six Music, 2001/Tree Publishing, 2001
Performed by Brooks and Dunn on the album *Steers & Stripes* (Arista Nashville, 2001).

Only Time
Words by Roma Ryan, music by Enya (pseudonym for Eithne Ni Bhraonain) and Nicky Ryan
EMI-Blackwood Music Inc., 2000
Performed by Enya on the album *A Day Without Rain* (Reprise, 2000).

Oochie Wally
Words and music by Michael Epps, Eugene Gray, Jabari Jones, Nas (pseudonym for Nasir Jones), and Lamont Porter
Big Horse Music, 2001/Ez Elpee Music, 2001/Our Write Music, 2001
Performed by QB Finest featuring Nas and Bravehearts on the album *Queensbridge: The Album* (Ill Will/Columbia, 2001).

Out of Nowhere
Words and music by Randall Barlow, Emilio Estefan, Jr., and Liza Quintana
Foreign Imported Productions, 2001
Performed by Gloria Estefan on the album *Greatest Hits, Vol. II* (Epic, 2001). Nominated for a Grammy Award, Best Dance Recording, 2001.

Overload
Words and music by Keisha Buchanan, Mutya Buena, Siobhan Donaghy, Felix Howard, Cameron MacVey, Johnny Rockstar, and Paul Simm
EMI-Blackwood Music Inc., 2001
Performed by the Sugarbabes on the album *One Touch* (London/Sire, 2001).

P

Papa's Got a Brand New Pigbag
Words and music by Rodger Freeman, music by Andrew Carpenter,
Simon Underwood, and James Johnstone
Mistral Entertainment Music, 1982/Warner Brothers Music Ltd., 1982
Covered by Thunderpuss. Released as a single (Tommy Boy, 2001).
Originally performed by Pigbag.

Parents Just Don't Understand
Words and music by Peter Harris, The Fresh Prince (pseudonym for
Willard Smith), and DJ Jazzy Jeff (pseudonym for Jeffrey Townes)
Jazzy Jeff & Fresh Prince, 1988/Zomba Enterprises, 1988
Covered by Lil' Romeo, Nick Cannon, and 3LW. Released as a single
(Jive, 2001). Originally performed by DJ Jazzy Jeff and the Fresh
Prince.

Part II
Words and music by Redman (pseudonym for Reggie Noble), Erick
Sermon, and Method Man (pseudonym for Clifford Smith), music by
Toni Braxton, Kenneth Edmonds, and Bryce Wilson
Careers-BMG Music, 2001/Ecaf Music, 2001/Jay Bird Alley Music,
2001/Lady Ashley Music, 2001/Sony ATV Songs LLC, 2001/Erick
Sermon Enterprises, 2001/Famous Music Corp., 2001/Funky Noble
Productions, 2001
Performed by Method Man and Redman on the movie soundtrack album
How High (Def Jam, 2001).

Pass It On
Music by David Aude and Da Silva Lopez
Clanger Songs, 2001/Egotrippin Music, 2001/Superstar Maker Music,
2001
Performed by Keoki on the album *Jealousy* (Moonshine, 2001).

Peaceful World
Words and music by John Mellencamp
Belmont Mall Publishing, 2001

Performed by John Mellencamp featuring India.Arie on the album *Cuttin' Heads* (Columbia, 2001). Nominated for a Grammy Award, Best Male Rock Vocal Performance, 2001.

Peaches & Cream
Words and music by Jason Boyd, Sean Combs, Daron Jones, Michael Keith, Quinnes Parker, Marvin Scandrick, Courtney Sills, and Mario Winans
C Sills Publishing, 2001/Da 12 Music, 2001/EMI-April Music, 2001/ Justin Combs Publishing, 2001/Janice Combs Music, 2001/Marsky Music, 2001
Performed by 112 on the album *Part III* (Bad Boy, 2001). Nominated for a Grammy Award, Best R&B Performance by a Duo or Group With Vocal, 2001.

Photograph
Words and music by Rivers Cuomo
E. O. Smith Music, 2001
Performed by Weezer on the album *Weezer* (Geffen, 2001).

Picture
Words and music by Sheryl Crow and Kid Rock (pseudonym for Robert Ritchie)
Old Crow Music, 2001/Thirty Two Mile Music, 2001/Warner-Tamerlane Publishing, 2001
Performed by Kid Rock featuring Sheryl Crow on the album *Cocky* (Lava/Atlantic, 2001).

Planets of the Universe
Words and music by Stevie Nicks
Welsh Witch Music, 1979
Performed by Stevie Nicks on the album *Trouble in Shangri-la* (Reprise, 2001). Nominated for a Grammy Award, Best Female Rock Vocal Performance, 2001.

Play
Words and music by Anders Bagge, Arnthor Birgisson, Christina Milian, and Mark Rooney
Cori Tiffani Publishing, 2001/Songs of Universal, 2001/Universal-MCA Music Publishing, 2001/Air Chrysalis Scandinavia, 2001/Murlyn Songs, 2001
Performed by Jennifer Lopez on the album *J.Lo* (Epic, 2001).

Po' Punch
Words and music by Lil' Jon and Roy Thorne
Pocket Change Publishing, 2000
Performed by Po' White Trash & the Trailer Park Symphony on the album *Po' Like Dis* (Pocket Change, 2001).

Poor Side of Town
Words and music by Johnny Rivers (pseudonym for John Ramistella)
and Lou Adler
EMI Sosaha Music, 1966/Jonathan Three Music, 1966
Covered by Nick Lowe on the album *The Convincer* (Yep Roc, 2001).
Originally performed by Johnny Rivers.

Pop
Words and music by Wade Robson and Justin Timberlake
Wajero Music, 2001/Tennman Tunes, 2001
Performed by *NSYNC on the album *Celebrity* (Jive, 2001).

Poultry in Motion
Music by Johnny Castle, William Kirchen, and Jack O'Dell
Lerocious Music, 2001
Performed by Bill Kirchen on the album *Tied to the Wheel* (HighTone,
2001). Nominated for a Grammy Award, Best Country Instrumental
Performance, 2001.

Pour Me
Words and music by Rory Beighley, Bryan Burns, Ira Dean, Heidi
Newfield, and Sam Harp
Rope & String Music, 2000/WB Music Publishing, 2000/Sammy Harpo
Music, 2000/Hapsack Music, 2000/Warner-Tamerlane Publishing,
2000
Performed by Trick Pony on the album *Trick Pony* (Warner Bros.,
2001).

The Power of One
Words and music by Mark Chait, John Loeffler, Ralph Schuckett, and
Mervyn Warren
Mewtwo Music, 2000/Tamarama Music, 2000/Two Twenty Nine Music,
2000/Vaporeon Music, 2000
Performed by Donna Summer on the movie soundtrack album *Pokemon
2000: The Power of One* (Atlantic, 2000).

Prison Song
Words and music by Daron Malakian, words by Serj Tankian, music by
Shavarsh Odadjian and John Dolmayan
Ddevil Music, 2001/Sony ATV Tunes LLC, 2001
Performed by System of a Down on the album *Toxicity* (American
Recordings, 2001).

Project Chick
Words and music by Dwayne Carter, Juvenile (pseudonym for Terius
Gray), Byron Thomas, and Bryan Williams
Breka Music, 2001/Money Mack Music, 2001

Performed by the Cash Money Millionaires. Released as a single (Cash Money/Universal, 2001).

Promise
Words and music by Brandon Casey, Brian Casey, Bryan Cox, Jermaine Dupri, Gary Smith, and Lechas Young

Air Control Music, 2001/EMI-April Music, 2001/So So Def Music, 2001/Them Damn Twins Music, 2001/Gizzo Music, 2001/Noontime South, 2001/W B M Music, 2001/Babyboys Little Pub Co, 2001

Performed by Jagged Edge featuring Jermaine Dupri and Loon. Released as a single (So So Def/Sony, 2001). Originally featured on the Jagged Edge album *J.E. Heartbreak* (So So Def/Sony, 1999).

Purple Pills
Words and music by Jeff Bass, Von Carlisle, DeShaun Holton, Rufus Johnson, Eminem (pseudonym for Marshall Mathers), Ondre Moore, and Denaun Porter

Eight Mile Style Music, 2001/EMI-Blackwood Music Inc., 2001/Ensign Music, 2001/Derty Werks, 2001/EMI-April Music, 2001/Idiotic Biz, 2001/Runyon Ave, 2001/Swifty McVay Publishing, 2001

Performed by D12 on the album *Devil's Night* (Shady/Interscope, 2001).

Put It on Me
Words and music by Ja Rule (pseudonym for Jeffrey Atkins), Tiheem Crocker, Irv Gotti (pseudonym for Irving Lorenzo), and Paul Walcott

Blunts Guns and Funds, 2000/Famous Music Corp., 2000/Tru Stylze Music, 2000/DJ Irv Publishing, 2000/Ensign Music, 2000/Slavery Music, 2000/Songs of Universal, 2000

Performed by Ja Rule featuring Lil' Mo and Vita on the album *Rule 3:36* (Def Jam, 2000). Nominated for a Grammy Award, Best Rap Performance by a Duo or Group, 2001.

R

Rain
Music by Christopher Maresh
Stalmach Music, 2000
Performed by Eric Johnson & Alien Love Child on the album *Live and
Beyond* (Favored Nations, 2000). Nominated for a Grammy Award,
Best Pop Instrumental Performance, 2001.

Rainbow Children
Words and music by Prince
Controversy Music, 2001
Performed by Prince on the album *The Rainbow Children* (Redline,
2001).

Raise Up
Words and music by Petey Pablo (pseudonym for Moses Barrett, III)
and Timbaland (pseudonym for Timothy Mosley)
Kumbaya, 2001/Virginia Beach Music, 2001/WB Music Publishing,
2001/Zomba Enterprises, 2001
Performed by Petey Pablo on the album *Diary of a Sinner: 1st Entry*
(Jive, 2001).

Re-Hash
Words and music by Damon Albarn and Jamie Hewlett
EMI-Blackwood Music Inc., 2000/EMI United Partnership Ltd.,
2000/WB Music Publishing, 2000
Performed by Gorillaz on the album *Gorillaz* (Virgin, 2001).

Real Life (I Never Was the Same Again)
Words and music by Jim Janoski and Joe Thrasher
Major Bob Music, 2001/Castrie Music, 2001/Whiskey Gap Music, 2001
Performed by Jeff Carson on the album *Real Life* (Curb, 2001).

Relax
Words and music by Peter Gill, Holly Johnson, and Mark O'Toole
SPZ Music, London, England, 1984/Perfect Songs Ltd., 1984

Covered by Powerman 5000 on the movie soundtrack album *Zoolander* (Hollywood, 2001). Originally performed by Frankie Goes to Hollywood on the album *Welcome to the Pleasuredome* (ZTT/Island, 1984).

Renegades of Funk
Words and music by Arthur Baker, John Robie, Afrika Bambaataa (pseudonym for Bambaataa Khayan Aasim), and John Miller
Shakin Baker Music, 1984/Bambaataa Music, 1984/T Girl Music LLC, 1984
Covered by Rage Against the Machine on the album *Renegades* (Epic, 2000). Originally performed by Afrika Bambaataa. Nominated for a Grammy Award, Best Hard Rock Performance, 2001.

Reptile
Music by Eric Clapton
EC Music Ltd., 2001/Unichappell Music Inc., 2001
Performed by Eric Clapton on the album *Reptile* (Reprise, 2001). Won a Grammy Award for Best Pop Instrumental Performance, 2001.

Request + Line
Words and music by William Adams, Michael Fratantuno, III, James Lawrence, Macy Gray (pseudonym for Natalie McIntyre), George Pajon, and Allan Pineda
Rhett Rhyme Music, 2001/El Cubano Music, 2001/Happy Mel Boopy's Cocktail Lounge, 2001/Jeepney Music Publishing, 2001/Tuono Music, 2001/Will I Am Music, 2001/Zomba Songs, 2001
Performed by Black Eyed Peas featuring Macy Gray on the album *Bridging the Gap* (Interscope, 2000).

Ride Wit Me
Words by Nelly (pseudonym for Cornell Haynes), music by Eldra DeBarge, William DeBarge, Jason Epperson, Etterlene Jordan, and Lovell Webb, Jr
BMG Songs Inc., 2000/D2 Pro Publishing, 2000/Jay E's Basement, 2000/Jobete Music Co., 2000/Universal-MCA Music Publishing, 2000/Dynacom Publishing, 2000/Songs of Universal, 2000
Performed by Nelly featuring City Spud on the album *Country Grammar* (Universal, 2000). Nominated for a Grammy Award, Best Rap Solo Performance, 2001.

Ridin'
Words and music by Jonathan Brightman, Devon Glenn, Keith Nelson, and Joshua Todd
Famous Music Corp., 2001/Lit Up Music, 2001
Performed by Buckcherry on the album *Time Bomb* (DreamWorks, 2001).

Riding With Private Malone
Words and music by Wood Newton and Thom Shepherd
Maximus Nashville, 2001/Twang Thang Music, 2001/LG Wells Music,
    2001/Wood and I Music, 2001
Performed by David Ball on the album *Amigo* (Dualtone, 2001).

Right Where I Need to Be
Words and music by Casey Beathard and Kendell Marvel
Acuff Rose Music, 1999/Big Yellow Dog Music, 1999/Six O One
    Broadway Music, 1999/Tree Publishing, 1999
Performed by Gary Allan on the album *Smoke Rings in the Dark* (MCA
    Nashville, 1999).

Rise
Words and music by Ian Astbury and Billy Duffy
Tayminster Ltd., 2001/Screenchoice Ltd., 2001
Performed by the Cult on the album *Beyond Good and Evil* (Lava/
    Atlantic, 2001).

Rock the Boat
Words and music by Stephen Garrett, Eric Seats, and Rapture Stewart
E Beats Music, 2001/Rap Tracks Publishing, 2001/WB Music
    Publishing, 2001/Black Fountain Music, 2001/Herbilicious Music,
    2001
Performed by Aaliyah on the album *Aaliyah* (Blackground, 2001).
    Nominated for a Grammy Award, Best Female R&B Vocal
    Performance, 2001.

Rock Show
Words and music by Christopher Davis, Stephan Jenkins, D.M.C.
    (pseudonym for Darryl McDaniels), and Run (pseudonym for Joseph
    Simmons)
EMI-Blackwood Music Inc., 2001/Three EB Publishing, 2001/EMI-April
    Music, 2001/Protoons Inc., 2001
Performed by Run-D.M.C. featuring Stephan Jenkins on the album
    Crown Royal (Arista, 2001).

The Rock Show
Words and music by Travis Barker, Thomas Delonge, and Mark Hoppus
EMI-April Music, 2001/Fun With Goats Music, 2001
Performed by Blink-182 on the album *Take Off Your Pants and Jacket*
    (MCA, 2001).

Rock Star
Words and music by Arthur Alexakis, music by Greg Eklund and Craig
    Montoya   .
Common Green Music, 2000/Evergleam Music, 2000/Irving Music Inc.,
    2000/Montalupis Music, 2000

Performed by Everclear on the movie soundtrack album *Rock Star* (Priority, 2001). Originally featured on the Everclear album *Songs From an American Movie, Vol. Two: Good Time for a Bad Attitude* (Capitol, 2000).

Rockin' the Suburbs
Words and music by Ben Folds
Free From the Man Songs, 2001
Performed by Ben Folds on the album *Rockin' the Suburbs* (Epic, 2001).

Romeo
Words and music by Felix Buxton and Simon Ratcliffe
Songs of Universal, 2001
Performed by Basement Jaxx on the album *Rooty* (Astralwerks, 2001).

Room 335
Music by Larry Carlton
Pal-Dog Music, 1978
Performed by Larry Carlton and Steve Lukather on the album *No Substitutions: Live in Osaka* (Favored Nations, 2001). Originally performed by Larry Carlton on the album *Larry Carlton* (Warner Bros., 1978). Nominated for a Grammy Award, Best Pop Instrumental Performance, 2001.

S

Safe in New York City
Words and music by Angus Young and Malcolm Young
J. Albert & Son Music, 2000
Performed by AC/DC on the album *Stiff Upper Lip* (Elektra, 2000).

San Antonio Girl
Words and music by Lyle Lovett
Universal-MCA Music Publishing, 2001
Performed by Lyle Lovett on the album *Anthology, Volume One: Cowboy Man* (MCA, 2001). Nominated for a Grammy Award, Best Male Country Vocal Performance, 2001.

Schism
Words and music by Daniel Carey, Justin Chancellor, Adam Jones, and Maynard Keenan
EMI-Virgin Music, 2001/Toolshed Music, 2001
Performed by Tool on the album *Lateralus* (Volcano, 2001). Won a Grammy Award for Best Metal Performance, 2001.

Second Wind
Words and music by Steve Leslie and Darryl Worley
EMI-Blackwood Music Inc., 2000
Performed by Darryl Worley on the album *Hard Rain Don't Last* (DreamWorks, 2000).

Set It Off
Words and music by Juvenile (pseudonym for Terius Gray) and Byron Thomas
Breka Music, 2001/Money Mack Music, 2001
Performed by Juvenile on the album *Project English* (Cash Money/ Universal, 2001).

Sexual Revolution
Words by Macy Gray (pseudonym for Natalie McIntyre), words and music by David Wilder, Jeremy Ruzumna, and Darryl Swann

D Style Music, 2001/EMI-April Music, 2001/Ooky Spinalton Music, 2001/Roastitoasti Music, 2001/Happy Mel Boopy's Cocktail Lounge, 2001/Zomba Songs, 2001
Performed by Macy Gray on the album *The Id* (Epic, 2001).

Shaniqua
Words by Little-T (pseudonym for Timothy Sullivan), music by One Track Mike (pseudonym for Michael Flannery)
WB Music Publishing, 2001
Performed by Little-T and One Track Mike on the album *Fome Is Dape* (Lava/Atlantic, 2001).

Shape of My Heart
Words and music by Lisa Miskovsky, Martin Sandberg, and Rami Yacoub
Universal Polygram International Pub., 2000/Zomba Enterprises, 2000
Performed by the Backstreet Boys on the album *Black & Blue* (Jive, 2000). Nominated for a Grammy Award, Best Pop Performance by a Duo or Group With Vocal, 2001.

She Couldn't Change Me
Words and music by Christopher Knight and Gary Nicholson
Roger Nichols Music Inc., 2001/Sony Tunes, 2001/WB Music Publishing, 2001
Performed by Montgomery Gentry on the album *Carrying On* (Columbia, 2001).

She Misses Him
Words and music by Tim Johnson
EMI-Blackwood Music Inc., 2001/Tim Johnson Music Publishing, 2001
Performed by Tim Rushlow on the album *Tim Rushlow* (Atlantic, 2001).

She's All I Got
Words and music by Mike City (pseudonym for Michael Flowers)
Mike City Music, 2001/Warner-Tamerlane Publishing, 2001
Performed by Jimmy Cozier on the album *Jimmy Cozier* (J Records, 2001).

Shine
Words and music by Edgar Roland
Sugarfuzz Music, 1994/Warner-Tamerlane Publishing, 1994
Covered by Dolly Parton on the album *Little Sparrow* (Sugar Hill, 2001). Originally performed by Collective Soul on the album *Hints, Allegations, and Things Left Unsaid* (Rising Storm, 1993). Won a Grammy Award for Best Female Country Vocal Performance, 2001.

Shit on You
Words and music by Von Carlisle, Rufus Johnson, Eminem (pseudonym for Marshall Mathers), Ondre Moore, and Denaun Porter, music by

Lonnie Smith
EMI-April Music, 2000/Idiotic Biz, 2000/Runyon Ave, 2000/Swifty
  McVay Publishing, 2000/Eight Mile Style Music, 2000/Screen Gems-
  EMI Music Inc., 2000
Performed by D12. Initially released as a single (Shady/Interscope,
  2000); later featured on the album *Devil's Night* (Shady/Interscope,
  2001).

Short Circuit
Music by Thomas Bangalter and Guy de Homem-Christo
Reach Global Songs, 2000/Ttuff Ttony Music, 2000/Zomba Songs, 2000
Performed by Daft Punk on the album *Discovery* (Virgin, 2001).
  Nominated for a Grammy Award, Best Pop Instrumental Performance,
  2001.

Short Skirt/Long Jacket
Words and music by John McCrea
EMI-Blackwood Music Inc., 2001/Stamen Music, 2001
Performed by Cake on the album *Comfort Eagle* (Columbia, 2001).

Simple Things
Words and music by James Brickman, Darrell Brown, and Beth Nielsen
  Chapman
BNC Songs, 2001/Grey Ink Music, 2001
Performed by Jim Brickman featuring Rebecca Lynn Howard on the
  album *Simple Things* (Windham Hill, 2001).

Sing
Words and music by Francis Healy
Sony ATV Songs LLC, 2001
Performed by Travis on the album *The Invisible Band* (Epic, 2001).

Six-Pack Summer
Words and music by Charles Black, Thomas Rocco, and Phillip Vassar
EMI-April Music, 2000/Milene Music, 2000/Phil Vassar Music, 2000/
  EMI-Blackwood Music Inc., 2000/Flybridge Tunes, 2000
Performed by Phil Vassar on the album *Phil Vassar* (Arista Nashville,
  2000).

Smooth Criminal
Words and music by Michael Jackson
Mijac Music, 1987
Covered by Alien Ant Farm on the album *ANThology* (DreamWorks,
  2001). Originally performed by Michael Jackson on the album *Bad*
  (Epic, 1987). Nominated for a Grammy Award, Best Hard Rock
  Performance, 2001.

So Fresh, So Clean
Words and music by Rico Wade, Andre Benjamin, Patrick Brown,

Raymon Murray, and Antwan Patton
Organized Noize Music, 2000/Chrysalis Music, 2000/Gnat Booty Music, 2000
Performed by Outkast on the album *Stankonia* (LaFace/Arista, 2000).

So in Love With Two
Words and music by Mikaila, Mikkel Eriksen, Tor Hermansen, and Hallgeir Rustan
EMI-April Music, 2001/Sony ATV Tunes LLC, 2001/Mika Magic Music, 2001
Performed by Mikaila. Initially released as a single (Polygram, 2000); later featured on the album *Mikaila* (Island, 2001).

Someone to Call My Lover
Words and music by Terry Lewis, James Harris, III, and Janet Jackson, music by Lee Bunnell
Black Ice Publishing, 2001/EMI-April Music, 2001/Flyte Tyme Tunes, 2001/WB Music Publishing, 2001
Performed by Janet Jackson on the album *All for You* (Virgin, 2001). Nominated for a Grammy Award, Best Female Pop Vocal Performance, 2001.

Soul Sista
Words and music by Bilal (pseudonym for Bilal Oliver), James Mtume, and Charlie Ray Wiggins
Jazzmen Publishing, 2000/Mtume Music, 2000/Warner-Tamerlane Publishing, 2000
Performed by Bilal. Initially released as a single (Interscope, 2000); later featured on the album *1st Born Second* (Interscope, 2001).

Souljas
Words and music by Master P (pseudonym for Percy Miller)
Big P Music, 2001
Performed by Master P on the album *Ghetto Postage* (No Limit/Priority, 2000).

South Side
Words and music by Moby (pseudonym for Richard Melville Hall)
Little Idiot Music, 1999/Warner-Tamerlane Publishing, 1999
Performed by Moby featuring Gwen Stefani on the album *Play* (V2, 1999).

Southern Hospitality
Words and music by Ludacris (pseudonym for Christopher Bridges) and Pharrell Williams
EMI-April Music, 2000/Ludacris Music Publishing, 2000/EMI-Blackwood Music Inc., 2000/Waters of Nazareth Publishing, 2000

Performed by Ludacris featuring Pharrell on the album *Back for the First Time* (Def Jam South, 2000).

The Space Between
Words and music by David Matthews and Glen Ballard
Aerostation Corp., 2000/Colden Grey Ltd., 2000/Universal-MCA Music Publishing, 2000
Performed by the Dave Matthews Band on the album *Everyday* (RCA, 2001). Nominated for a Grammy Award, Best Rock Performance by a Duo or Group With Vocal, 2001.

Squares
Words and music by Richard Greentree, Robin Jones, David MacLean, and Stephen Mason, music by Sylveer Vanholme and Raymond Vincent
Beechwood Music, 2001/EMI-Blackwood Music Inc., 2001
Performed by the Beta Band on the album *Hot Shots II* (Astralwerks, 2001).

Start the Commotion
Words and music by Robert Bogle, Salaam Gibbs, Theo Keating, Greg Mays, Melvin Taylor, and Donald Wilson
EMI-April Music, 1999/Salaam Remi Music, 1999/EMI Unart Catalogue, 1999
Performed by the Wiseguys on the movie soundtrack album *Zoolander* (Hollywood, 2001). Originally featured on the Wiseguys album *The Antidote* (Wall of Sound, 1998).

Still
Words and music by Brian McKnight and Brandon Barnes
Universal Polygram International Pub., 2001/Brandon Barnes Music, 2001/Universal Songs of Polygram Intntl., 2001
Performed by Brian McKnight on the album *Superhero* (Motown, 2001). Nominated for a Grammy Award, Best Male Pop Vocal Performance, 2001.

Strange Condition
Words and music by Peter Yorn
Boyletown Music, 2000
Performed by Pete Yorn on the album *Musicforthemorningafter* (Columbia, 2001). Originally featured on the movie soundtrack album *Me, Myself & Irene* (Elektra/Asylum, 2000).

Strange Little Girl
Words and music by Jean Jacques Burnel, Hugh Cornwell, Brian Duffy, David Greenfield, and Hans Warmling
Incomplete Music, 1982/Plumbshaft Ltd., 1982
Covered by Tori Amos on the album *Strange Little Girls* (Atlantic,

2001). Originally performed by the Stranglers. Nominated for a Grammy Award, Best Female Rock Vocal Performance, 2001.

Stranger in My House
Words and music by Anthony Crawford and Shae Jones
Shae Shae Music, 2000/Shep and Shep Publishing, 2000
Performed by Tamia on the album *A Nu Day* (Elektra, 2000).

Stuck in a Moment You Can't Get Out Of
Words and music by Bono (pseudonym for Paul Hewson) and The Edge (pseudonym for David Evans), music by Larry Mullen, Jr. and Adam Clayton
Universal Polygram International Pub., 2000
Performed by U2 on the album *All That You Can't Leave Behind* (Interscope, 2000). Won a Grammy Award for Best Pop Performance by a Duo or Group With Vocal, 2001. Nominated for a Grammy Award, Song of the Year, 2001.

Stuck in My Car
Words and music by Charlotte Caffey, Peter Stuart, and Jane Wiedlin
Chargo Music, 2001/Wiedwacker Music, 2001/EMI-Virgin Songs, 2001/ Loud Mouse Music, 2001
Performed by the Go-Go's on the album *God Bless the Go-Go's* (Beyond, 2001).

Stutter
Words and music by Ernest Dixon and Roy Hamilton
Platinum Firm Music, 2000/Zomba Enterprises, 2000/Zomba Songs, 2000
Performed by Joe featuring Mystikal. Released as a single (Jive, 2001).

Sugarfoot Rag
Music by Hank Garland, words by George Vaughn
Hollis Music Inc., 1949/Unichappell Music Inc., 1949
Covered by Asleep at the Wheel featuring Brad Paisley on the album *The Very Best of Asleep at the Wheel* (Relentless, 2001). Originally performed by Hank Garland. Nominated for a Grammy Award, Best Country Instrumental Performance, 2001.

Superman Inside
Words and music by Doyle Bramhall, II, Eric Clapton, and Susannah Melvoin
EC Music Ltd., 2001/Unichappell Music Inc., 2001/Wirzma Publishing, 2001/Bug Music, 2001/Chrysalis Music, 2001
Performed by Eric Clapton on the album *Reptile* (Reprise, 2001). Nominated for a Grammy Award, Best Male Rock Vocal Performance, 2001.

Superman (It's Not Easy)

Words and music by John Ondrasik

EMI-Blackwood Music Inc., 2000/Five for Fighting Music, 2000

Performed by Five for Fighting on the album *America Town* (Columbia, 2000). Nominated for a Grammy Award, Best Pop Performance by a Duo or Group With Vocal, 2001.

Superwoman Pt. II

Words by Fabolous (pseudonym for John Jackson) and Lil' Mo (pseudonym for Cynthia Loving), music by Kenneth Ifill and Ernesto Shaw

Duro Music, 2001/EMI-Blackwood Music Inc., 2001/Mr. Manatti Music, 2001/J Brasco, 2001/Mo Loving Music, 2001

Performed by Lil' Mo featuring Fabolous on the album *Based on a True Story* (Elektra, 2001).

Survivor

Words and music by Anthony Dent, Beyonce Knowles, and Matthew Knowles

Beyonce Publishing, 2001/For Chase Muzic, 2001/Hitco South, 2001/M W E Publishing, 2001/Sony ATV Tunes LLC, 2001

Performed by Destiny's Child on the album *Survivor* (Columbia, 2001). Won a Grammy Award for Best R&B Performance by a Duo or Group With Vocal, 2001.

Sweet Baby

Words by Macy Gray (pseudonym for Natalie McIntyre), music by Joe Solo

Children of the Forest Music, 1998/Mel Boopie Music, 1998/Olos Eoj Publishing, 1998

Performed by Macy Gray featuring Erykah Badu on the album *The Id* (Epic, 2001).

T

Take It to Da House
Words and music by Corey Evans, Mark Seymour, Katrina Taylor,
Trick Daddy (pseudonym for Maurice Young), and Adam Duggins,
music by Charles Bobbit, James Brown, Harry Casey, and Fred
Wesley
Donna Dijon Music, 2001/Dynatone Publishing, 2001/EMI Longitude
Music, 2001/First and Gold Publishing, 2001/Universal-MCA Music
Publishing, 2001
Performed by Trick Daddy featuring Slip-N-Slide Express on the album
Thugs Are Us (Atlantic, 2001).

Take the Money and Run
Words and music by Steve Miller
Sailor Music, 1976
Covered by Run-D.M.C. featuring Everlast on the album *Crown Royal*
(Arista, 2001). Originally performed by the Steve Miller Band on the
album *Fly Like an Eagle* (Capitol, 1976).

Take You Out
Words and music by Warryn Campbell, Harold Lilly, and John Smith
Dango Music, 2001/EMI-April Music, 2001/Nyrraw Music, 2001/EMI-
Blackwood Music Inc., 2001/Uncle Bobby Music, 2001
Performed by Luther Vandross on the album *Luther Vandross* (J
Records, 2001).

Tell Me Who
Words and music by Anthony Crawford and Tamia
Almo Music Corp., 2000/Hudson Jordan Music, 2000/Plus 1 Publishing,
2000
Performed by Tamia on the album *A Nu Day* (Elektra, 2000).

Thank You in Advance
Words and music by Anthony Crawford
Almo Music Corp., 2000/Hudson Jordan Music, 2000

Performed by Boyz II Men on the album *Nathan Michael Shawn Wanya* (Universal, 2000).

Thanks That Was Fun
Words and music by Steven Page and Ed Robertson
Treat Baker Music, 2001/WB Music Publishing, 2001
Performed by the Barenaked Ladies on the album *Disc One: All Their Greatest Hits, 1991<en>2001* (Reprise, 2001).

That's How I Beat Shaq
Words and music by Brian Kierulf and Joshua Schwartz
Kierulf Songs, 2000/Mugsy Boy Publishing, 2000/Zomba Songs, 2000
Performed by Aaron Carter on the album *Aaron's Party (Come Get It)* (Jive, 2000).

There Is No Arizona
Words and music by Lisa Drew, Jamie O'Neal (pseudonym for Jamie Murphy), and Shaye Smith
EMI-April Music, 2000/Jersey Girl Music, 2000/EMI-Blackwood Music Inc., 2000/Mark Alan Springer Music, 2000
Performed by Jamie O'Neal on the album *Shiver* (Polygram, 2000). Nominated for Grammy Awards, Best Country Song, 2001, and Best Female Country Vocal Performance, 2001.

There It Is
Words and music by Marcus Clinkscale, Harold Garvin, Clifton Jones, Ginuwine (pseudonym for Elgin Lumpkin), Bobby Terry, Jerry Vines, Isaac Wiley, and Curtis Williams
Kling Kling Music, 2001/Music of Windswept, 2001/5700 Park Music, 2001/Bob D Terry Publishing, 2001/EMI-Blackwood Music Inc., 2001
Performed by Ginuwine on the album *The Life* (Epic, 2001).

There She Goes
Words and music by Babyface (pseudonym for Kenneth Edmonds), Charles Hugo, and Pharrell Williams
Chase Chad Music, 2001/EMI-April Music, 2001/Ecaf Music, 2001/EMI-Blackwood Music Inc., 2001/Sony ATV Songs LLC, 2001/Waters of Nazareth Publishing, 2001
Performed by Babyface on the album *Face2Face* (Arista, 2001).

There You'll Be
Words and music by Diane Warren
Realsongs, 2001/Touchstone Pictures Music and Songs, 2001
Performed by Faith Hill in the movie and on the soundtrack album *Pearl Harbor* (Warner Bros., 2001). Nominated for an Academy Award, Best Original Song, 2001;~ Nominated for an Academy Award, Best Original Song, 2001;~ Grammy Awards, Best Female

Pop Vocal Performance, 2001, and Best Song Written for a Motion Picture/Television, 2001.

There You'll Be
Words and music by Diane Warren
Realsongs, 2001/Touchstone Pictures Music and Songs, 2001
Performed by Kirk Whalum on the album *Unconditional* (Warner Bros., 2001). Nominated for a Grammy Award, Best Pop Instrumental Performance, 2001.

This Everyday Love
Words and music by Gene Nelson and Danny Wells
Irving Music Inc., 2000/Emelia Music, 2000
Performed by Rascal Flatts on the album *Rascal Flatts* (Lyric Street, 2000).

This I Promise You
Words and music by Richard Marx
Chi-Boy Music, 2000
Performed by *NSYNC on the album *No Strings Attached* (Jive, 2000).

This Is Love
Words and music by Polly Jean Harvey
EMI-Blackwood Music Inc., 2000
Performed by PJ Harvey on the album *Stories From the City, Stories From the Sea* (Island, 2000). Later featured on the movie soundtrack album *Jay and Silent Bob Strike Back* (Universal, 2001). Nominated for a Grammy Award, Best Female Rock Vocal Performance, 2001.

This Is Me
Words and music by David Frank, Stephen Kipner, and Pamela Sheyne
Warner-Tamerlane Publishing, 2001/Griff Griff Music, 2001/Sonic Grafitti, 2001/EMI-April Music, 2001/Stephen A. Kipner Music, 2001/Appletree Songs, 2001
Performed by Dream on the album *It Was All a Dream* (Bad Boy, 2001).

This Is Where I Came In
Words and music by Robin Gibb, Barry Gibb, and Maurice Gibb
Gibb Brothers Music, 2001
Performed by the Bee Gees on the album *This Is Where I Came In* (Universal, 2001).

To Be Able to Love
Words and music by Andreas Carlsson and Kristian Lundin
Zomba Enterprises, 2001
Performed by Jessica Folker on the movie soundtrack album *On the Line* (Jive, 2001).

To Quote Shakespeare
Words and music by Greg Barnhill and Mary Lamar
Greg Barnhill Music, 2001/Platinum Plow, 2001/WB Music Publishing, 2001
Performed by the Clark Family Experience. Released as a single to radio stations only.

Too Bad
Words and music by Chad Kroeger, Michael Kroeger, Ryan Peake, and Ryan Vikedal
Warner-Tamerlane Publishing, 2001
Performed by Nickelback on the album *Silver Side Up* (Roadrunner, 2001).

Too Far From Texas
Words and music by Stephen Booker and Sandy Stewart
BMG Songs Inc., 2001/Songs of Windswept Pacific, 2001
Performed by Stevie Nicks featuring Natalie Maines on the album *Trouble in Shangri-la* (Reprise, 2001).

Tribute
Words and music by Jack Black and Kyle Gass
Buttflap Music, 2001/Time For My Breakfast, 2001
Performed by Tenacious D on the album *Tenacious D* (Epic, 2001).

Turn Off the Light
Words and music by Nelly Furtado
Nelstar Publishing, 2000
Performed by Nelly Furtado on the album *Whoa, Nelly!* (DreamWorks, 2000).

Turning Over
Words and music by Dan Bern
Kababa Music, Los Angeles, 2001
Performed by Dan Bern on the album *New American Language* (Messenger, 2001).

Tweedle Dee & Tweedle Dum
Words and music by Bob Dylan (pseudonym for Robert Zimmerman)
Special Rider Music, 2001
Performed by Bob Dylan on the album *Love and Theft* (Columbia, 2001).

Two People Fell in Love
Words and music by Brad Paisley, John Lovelace, and Tim Owens
EMI-April Music, 2001/Love Ranch Music, 2001/Sea Gayle Music, 2001
Performed by Brad Paisley on the album *Part II* (Arista Nashville, 2001).

U

U Got It Bad
Words and music by Usher, Bryan Cox, and Jermaine Dupri
EMI-April Music, 2001/So So Def Music, 2001/UR-IV Music, 2001/
    Babyboys Little Pub Co, 2001/Noontime South, 2001
Performed by Usher on the album *8701* (Arista, 2001).

U Make My Sun Shine
Words and music by Prince
Controversy Music, 2001
Performed by Prince and Angie Stone. Released as a single (Wingspan,
    2001).

U Remind Me
Words and music by Edmund Clement and Anita McCloud
Butterman Land Publishing, 2001/Elsie Louise Pitts Music, 2001/
    Smooth C Publishing, 2001/Songs of Universal, 2001/Songs of
    Windswept Pacific, 2001
Performed by Usher on the album *8701* (Arista, 2001). Won a Grammy
    Award for Best Male R&B Vocal Performance, 2001.

Ugly
Words and music by Bubba Sparxxx (pseudonym for Warren Mathis),
    Timbaland (pseudonym for Timothy Mosley), and Missy Elliott
EMI-Blackwood Music Inc., 2001/Two Hundred Miles From
    Civilization, 2001/Mass Confusion Productions, 2001/Virginia Beach
    Music, 2001/WB Music Publishing, 2001
Performed by Bubba Sparxxx featuring Missy Elliott on the album *Dark
    Days, Bright Nights* (Interscope, 2001).

Uhhnnhh
Words and music by Dominick Lamb, Corey Pierson, and J. White
Teamsta Entertainment Music, 2001
Performed by the Bad Seed. Released as a single (Rawkus, 2001).

Unforgiven
Words and music by Billie Joe Armstrong, Charlotte Caffey, and Jane
    Wiedlin
Green Daze Music, San Rafael, 2001/Chargo Music, 2001/WB Music
    Publishing, 2001/Wiedwacker Music, 2001
Performed by the Go-Go's featuring Billie Joe Armstrong on the album
    God Bless the Go-Go's (Beyond, 2001).

Until
Words and music by Sting (pseudonym for Gordon Sumner)
EMI-Blackwood Music Inc., 2001
Performed by Sting in the movie *Kate & Leopold*. Nominated for an
    Academy Award, Best Original Song, 2001.

Until the End of Time
Words and music by Steven George, Johnny Lee Jackson, John Lang,
    Richard Page, and 2Pac (pseudonym for Tupac Shakur)
Ali-Aja Music, 2001/Black Hispanic Music, 2001/BMG Songs Inc.,
    2001/Indolent Sloth Music, 2001/Panola Park Music, 2001/WB Music
    Publishing, 2001
Performed by 2Pac on the album *Until the End of Time* (Interscope,
    2001).

Used to Love
Words and music by Stephen Huff
Tuff Huff Music, 2001/Zomba Songs, 2001
Performed by Keke Wyatt on the album *Soul Sista* (MCA, 2001).

V

Vampires
Music by Robbie Merrill and Sully (pseudonym for Salvatore Erna)
Meeengya Music, 2000/Forces Beyond Productions, 2000/Jogar Music
  Publishing, 2000
Performed by Godsmack on the album *Awake* (Republic/Universal,
  2000). Nominated for a Grammy Award, Best Rock Instrumental
  Performance, 2001.

Vanilla Sky
Words and music by Paul McCartney
MPL Communications, 2001
Performed by Paul McCartney on the movie soundtrack album *Vanilla
  Sky* (Warner Bros., 2001). Nominated for an Academy Award, Best
  Original Song, 2001.

Video
Words and music by India Arie, Carlos Broady, and Reginald Hargis
Lastrada Music, 2001/WB Music Publishing, 2001/Good High Music,
  2001/Famous Music Corp., 2001/Six July Publishing, 2001/Warner-
  Tamerlane Publishing, 2001/Gold and Iron Music Publishing, 2001/
  Ensign Music, 2001
Performed by India.Arie on the album *Acoustic Soul* (Motown, 2001).
  Nominated for Grammy Awards, Best Female R&B Vocal
  Performance, 2001, Best R&B Song, 2001, Record of the Year, 2001,
  and Song of the Year, 2001.

V.I.P.
Words and music by Iggy Pop (pseudonym for James Osterberg),
  Whitey Kirst, Mooseman (pseudonym for Lloyd Roberts), and Alex
  Kirst
Thousand Mile Inc., 2001/Christ & Co., 2001/Bug Music, 2001
Performed by Iggy Pop on the album *Beat Em Up* (Virgin, 2001).

Visions of Paradise
Words and music by Matt Clifford, Mick Jagger, and Robert Thomas

95

Bidnis Inc., 2001/EMI-Blackwood Music Inc., 2001/Jagged Music, 2001
Performed by Mick Jagger on the album *Goddess in the Doorway*
  (Virgin, 2001).

W

W

Words and music by M. Ludlum, J. Green, L. Palmer, and M. Lavella

Rude Gal Music, 2001/Bleedy Eyes Music, 2001/Who Owns Your Music, 2001

Performed by Mystic featuring Planet Asia on the album *Cuts for Luck and Scars for Freedom* (GoodVibe, 2001). Nominated for a Grammy Award, Best Rap/Sung Collaboration, 2001.

Wait

Words and music by Jason Ross

Las Chivas Music, 2001

Performed by Seven Mary Three on the album *The Economy of Sound* (Mammoth, 2001).

Wait a Minute

Words and music by Charles Hugo, Lil' Kim (pseudonym for Kim Jones), and Pharrell Williams

Chase Chad Music, 2001/EMI-April Music, 2001/EMI-Blackwood Music Inc., 2001/Notorious Kim Music, 2001/Undeas Music, 2001/ Warner-Tamerlane Publishing, 2001/Waters of Nazareth Publishing, 2001

Performed by Ray J featuring Lil' Kim on the album *This Ain't a Game* (Atlantic, 2001).

Walk On

Words and music by Bono (pseudonym for Paul Hewson), music by The Edge (pseudonym for David Evans), Larry Mullen, Jr., and Adam Clayton

Universal Polygram International Pub., 2000

Performed by U2 on the album *All That You Can't Leave Behind* (Interscope, 2000). Won a Grammy Award for Record of the Year, 2001. Nominated for a Grammy Award, Best Rock Song, 2001.

Warning

Words and music by Billie Joe Armstrong, music by Mike Dirnt

(pseudonym for Mike Pritchard) and Tre Cool (pseudonym for Frank Wright, III)
Green Daze Music, San Rafael, 2000/WB Music Publishing, 2000
Performed by Green Day on the album *Warning* (Reprise, 2000).

The Way
Words and music by Andre Harris and Jill Scott
Blue's Baby Music, 2000/Dirty Dre Music, 2000/Jat Cat Music Publishing, 2000
Performed by Jill Scott on the album *Who Is Jill Scott? Words and Sounds, Vol. 1* (Hidden Beach/Epic, 2000).

We Come 1
Words and music by Maxwell Fraser, Rowland Armstrong, and Ayalah Bentovim
BMG Songs Inc., 2001/EMI-April Music, 2001/WB Music Publishing, 2001
Performed by Faithless on the album *Outrospective* (Arista, 2001).

We Need a Resolution
Words and music by Stephen Garrett and Timbaland (pseudonym for Timothy Mosley)
Black Fountain Music, 2001/Herbilicious Music, 2001/Virginia Beach Music, 2001/WB Music Publishing, 2001
Performed by Aaliyah featuring Timbaland on the album *Aaliyah* (Blackground, 2001).

Weapon of Choice
Words by Bootsy Collins, music by Fatboy Slim (pseudonym for Norman Cook) and Ashley Slater
Mashamug Music, 2000/Sony ATV Songs LLC, 2000/Universal Songs of Polygram Intntl., 2000/Universal Polygram International Pub., 2000
Performed by Fatboy Slim featuring Bootsy Collins on the album *Halfway Between the Gutter and the Stars* (Astralwerks, 2000). Won a Grammy Award for Best Short Form Music Video, 2001.

What Am I Gonna Do
Words and music by Joe Carter, Tyrese, and Trevor Job
BMG Songs Inc., 2001/Zovektion Music, 2001/Ensign Music, 2001/Harrindur Publishing, 2001/TJ Beats Publishing, 2001/Uncle Jake's Music, 2001
Performed by Tyrese on the album *2000 Watts* (RCA, 2001).

What I Really Meant to Say
Words and music by Christopher Dunn, Tommy James, and Cyndi Thomson
Cross Keys Publishing, 1999/Chris Waters Music, 1999/Still Working for the Man Music, 1999/Tommy Lee James Songs, 1999/Tree

Publishing, 1999
Performed by Cyndi Thomson on the album *My World* (Capitol, 2001).

What It Feels Like for a Girl
Words and music by Madonna (pseudonym for Madonna Ciccone) and
Guy Sigsworth
Universal Polygram International Pub., 2000/WB Music Publishing,
2000/Webo Girl Publishing, 2000
Performed by Madonna on the album *Music* (Maverick/Warner Bros.,
2000).

What It Is
Words and music by Busta Rhymes (pseudonym for Trevor Smith),
Charles Hugo, and Pharrell Williams
Chase Chad Music, 2001/EMI-April Music, 2001
Performed by Busta Rhymes featuring Kelis on the album *Genesis* (J
Records, 2001). Also featured on the various-artists album *Violator:
The Album, V2.0* (Violator/Loud, 2001).

What Would You Do
Words and music by Robert Pardlo and Maurice Toby
EMI-April Music, 2001/Pladis Music, 2001
Performed by City High on the album *City High* (Interscope, 2001).
Nominated for a Grammy Award, Best R&B Performance by a Duo
or Group With Vocal, 2001.

What's It Gonna Be?
Words and music by Kandice Love and Troy Oliver
Songs of Universal, 2001/Zollia Publishing, 2001/Sony ATV Tunes
LLC, 2001/Chocolate Factory Music, 2001
Performed by Jessica Simpson on the album *Irresistible* (Columbia,
2001).

When God-Fearin' Women Get the Blues
Words and music by Leslie Satcher (pseudonym for Leslie Winn)
Satcher Songs, 2001/Sony Tunes, 2001
Performed by Martina McBride on the album *Greatest Hits* (RCA,
2001).

When I Think About Angels
Words and music by Roxie Dean, Jamie O'Neal (pseudonym for Jamie
Murphy), and Lonnie Tillis
Warner-Tamerlane Publishing, 2000/EMI-April Music, 2000/Maverick
Music, 2000/Pang Toon Music, 2000/WB Music Publishing, 2000
Performed by Jamie O'Neal on the album *Shiver* (Polygram, 2000).
Nominated for a Grammy Award, Best Country Song, 2001.

When It All Goes South
Words and music by Charles Carnes, Janis Carnes, and John Jarvis

Cross Keys Publishing, 2001/Songs of Peer, 2001
Performed by Alabama on the album *When It All Goes South* (RCA
   Nashville, 2001).

When It's Over
Words and music by Mark McGrath, Rodney Sheppard, Matthew
   Karges, Craig Bullock, Charles Frazier, and David Kahne
E Equals Music, 2001/Grave Lack of Talent Music, 2001/Warner-
   Tamerlane Publishing, 2001
Performed by Sugar Ray on the album *Sugar Ray* (Lava/Atlantic, 2001).

When Somebody Loves You
Words and music by Alan Jackson
WB Music Publishing, 2000/Yee Haw Music, 2000
Performed by Alan Jackson on the album *When Somebody Loves You*
   (Arista Nashville, 2000).

When You Come Back Down
Words and music by Timothy O'Brien and Daniel O'Keefe
Howdy Skies Music, 1997/Universal-MCA Music Publishing, 1997/
   Bicameral Songs, 1997/Mighty Nice Music, 1997
Covered by Nickel Creek on the album *Nickel Creek* (Sugar Hill, 2000).
   Originally performed by Tim O'Brien on the album *When No One's
   Around* (Sugar Hill, 1997).

Where the Blacktop Ends
Words and music by James Shamblin and Steven Wariner
Built on Rock Music, 1999/Steve Wariner Music, 1999
Performed by Keith Urban on the album *Keith Urban* (Capitol
   Nashville, 1999).

Where I Come From
Words and music by Alan Jackson
WB Music Publishing, 2000/Yee Haw Music, 2000
Performed by Alan Jackson on the album *When Somebody Loves You*
   (Arista Nashville, 2000).

Where the Party At
Words and music by Brandon Casey, Brian Casey, Bryan Cox, Nelly
   (pseudonym for Cornell Haynes), and Jermaine Dupri
BMG Songs Inc., 2001/EMI-April Music, 2001/So So Def Music, 2001/
   Them Damn Twins Music, 2001/Babyboys Little Pub Co, 2001/
   Noontime South, 2001/W B M Music, 2001
Performed by Jagged Edge featuring Nelly on the album *Jagged Little
   Thrill* (So So Def/Sony, 2001). Nominated for a Grammy Award,
   Best Rap/Sung Collaboration, 2001.

Where the Stars and Stripes and the Eagle Fly
Words and music by Kenny Beard, Casey Beathard, and Aaron Tippin

Acuff Rose Music, 2001/Milene Music, 2001
Performed by Aaron Tippin. Released as a single (Lyric Street, 2001).

While You Loved Me
Words and music by Kim Williams, Mary Dodson, and Danny Wells
Irving Music Inc., 2000/Cross Keys Publishing, 2000/Kim Williams, 2000
Performed by Rascal Flatts on the album *Rascal Flatts* (Lyric Street, 2000).

Whispering a Prayer
Music by Steve Vai
Sy Vy Music, 2001
Performed by Steve Vai on the album *Alive in an Ultra World* (Epic, 2001). Nominated for a Grammy Award, Best Rock Instrumental Performance, 2001.

Who the Hell Are You?
Words and music by Vernon Burch, April Coates, Howard Redmon, and Andrew Van Dorsselaer
Rick's Music Inc., 2000/Sand B Music, 2000/Universal-MCA Music Publishing, 2000
Performed by Madison Avenue on the album *The Polyester Embassy* (Columbia, 2000).

Who I Am
Words and music by James Brett and Troy Verges
Songs of Teracel, 2000/Songs of Universal, 2000/Tree Publishing, 2000
Performed by Jessica Andrews on the album *Who I Am* (DreamWorks, 2001).

Who We Be
Words and music by Mickey Davis and DMX (pseudonym for Earl Simmons)
Fifty Four Vill Music, 2001
Performed by DMX on the album *The Great Depression* (Def Jam, 2001). Nominated for a Grammy Award, Best Rap Solo Performance, 2001.

Who's That Girl
Words and music by Eve (pseudonym for Eve Jeffers), Darrin Dean, Sheldon Harris, and Ignatius Jackson
Blondie Rockwell Music, 2001/Dead Game Publishing, 2001/Icepickjay Publishing, 2001/Teflon Hitz, 2001
Performed by Eve on the album *Scorpion* (Interscope, 2001).

Why They Call It Falling
Words and music by Roxie Dean and Donald Schlitz
Maverick Music, 2000/New Don Songs, 2000/New Hayes Music,

2000/WB Music Publishing, 2000
Performed by Lee Ann Womack on the album *I Hope You Dance* (MCA Nashville, 2000).

Win
Words and music by Brian McKnight and Brandon Barnes
Brandon Barnes Music, 2000/Fox Film Music Corp., 2000/Universal Songs of Polygram Intntl., 2000
Performed by Brian McKnight on the movie soundtrack album *Men of Honor* (Motown, 2000). Nominated for a Grammy Award, Best Song Written for a Motion Picture/Television, 2001.

Wish You Were Here
Words and music by Brandon Boyd, Michael Einziger, Dirk Lance (pseudonym for Alex Katunich), DJ Kilmore (pseudonym for Christopher Kilmore), and Jose Pasillas
EMI-April Music, 2001/Hunglikeyora, 2001
Performed by Incubus on the album *Morning View* (Immortal/Epic, 2001).

Without You
Words and music by Traci Hale, Orenthal Harper, Thabiso Nkhereanye, Phillip Stewart, and Katrina Willis
Breezeville Music Publishing, 2000/Hitco South, 2000/O J Harper Publishing, 2000/Silliwak, 2000/Songs of Peer, 2000/Hale Yeah Music, 2000/Tabulous Music, 2000
Performed by Charlie Wilson on the album *Bridging the Gap* (Interscope, 2000).

The Wizard
Words and music by Terence Butler, Ozzy Osbourne, and William Ward
Essex Music International, New York, 1970
Performed by Black Sabbath on the various-artists album *Ozzfest 2001: The S econd Millennium* (Epic, 2001). Originally featured on the Black Sabbath alb um *Black Sabbath* (Warner Bros., 1970). Nominated for a Grammy Award, Best Metal Performance, 2001.

The World's Greatest
Words and music by R. Kelly
R. Kelly Publishing, 2001/Zomba Songs, 2001
Performed by R. Kelly on the movie soundtrack album *Ali* (Interscope, 2001).

Wrapped Up in You
Words and music by Wayne Kirkpatrick
Sell the Cow Music, 1997/Warner-Tamerlane Publishing, 1997
Covered by Garth Brooks on the album *Scarecrow* (Capitol, 2001).

Originally performed by Wayne Kirkpatrick on the album *The Maple Room* (Rocketown, 2000).

www.Memory
Words and music by Alan Jackson
WB Music Publishing, 2000/Yee Haw Music, 2000
Performed by Alan Jackson on the album *When Somebody Loves You* (Arista Nashville, 2000).

Y

Yellow
Words and music by Guy Berryman, Jonathan Buckland, William
  Champion, and Christopher Martin
BMG Songs Inc., 2000
Performed by Coldplay on the album *Parachutes* (Nettwerk, 2000).
  Nominated for Grammy Awards, Best Rock Performance by a Duo or
  Group With Vocal, 2001, and Best Rock Song, 2001.

Yer Selfish Ways
Words and music by Christopher Gunst, Brent Rademaker, David Scher,
  and Aaron Sperske
Bucket Songs, 2001/Dugong Songs, 2001/Silverback Music, 2001/X Flat
  Minor Music, 2001
Performed by the Beachwood Sparks on the album *Once We Were Trees*
  (Sub Pop, 2001).

You Gets No Love
Words and music by Faith Evans, Mechalie Jamison, Michael
  Saulsberry, Andre Wilson, Kameelah Williams, and Toni Coleman
EMI-April Music, 2001/Gloria's Boy Music, 2001/Haleem Music, 2001/
  Justin Combs Publishing, 2001/Michael Angelo Saulsberry Music,
  2001/Chyna Baby Music, 2001/EMI-Blackwood Music Inc., 2001/
  Janice Combs Music, 2001/Wil Coll Publishing, 2001
Performed by Faith Evans featuring P. Diddy and Loon on the album
  Faithfully (Bad Boy, 2001).

You Rock My World
Words and music by Michael Jackson, LaShawn Daniels, Fred Jerkins,
  III, Rodney Jerkins, and Nora Payne
Generation 3rd Music, London, England, 2001/EMI-Blackwood Music
  Inc., 2001/Ensign Music, 2001/Fred Jerkins Publishing, 2001/Mijac
  Music, 2001/Rodney Jerkins Productions, 2001/EMI-April Music,
  2001
Performed by Michael Jackson on the album *Invincible* (Epic, 2001).

Nominated for a Grammy Award, Best Male Pop Vocal Performance, 2001.

You Shouldn't Kiss Me Like This
Words and music by Toby Keith (pseudonym for Toby Covel)
Tokeco Tunes, 1999
Performed by Toby Keith on the album *How Do You Like Me Now?!* (DreamWorks, 1999).

You and Whose Army?
Words and music by Colin Greenwood, Jonathan Greenwood, Edward O'Brien, Philip Selway, and Thomas Yorke
Warner-Chappell Music, 2001
Performed by Radiohead on the album *Amnesiac* (Capitol, 2001).

You Wouldn't Believe
Words and music by Nicholas Hexum and Douglas Martinez
Hydroponic Music, 2001
Performed by 311 on the album *From Chaos* (Volcano, 2001).

Your Disease
Words and music by Josey Scott (pseudonym for Joseph Sappington), music by Paul Crosby, Christopher Dabaldo, David Novotny, and Wayne Swinny
Almo Music Corp., 2001/Five Superstars, 2001
Performed by Saliva on the album *Every Six Seconds* (Island/Def Jam, 2001). Nominated for a Grammy Award, Best Hard Rock Performance, 2001.

Your Song
Words by Bernard Taupin, music by Elton John (pseudonym for Reginald Dwight)
Universal Songs of Polygram Intntl., 1970
Covered by Ewan McGregor and Alessandro Safina on the movie soundtrack album *Moulin Rouge* (Interscope, 2001). Originally performed by Elton John.

You're All I Need
Words and music by James Harris, III, Terry Lewis, Tony Tolbert, and James Wright
Ella and Gene's Son's Music, 2001/EMI-April Music, 2001/Flyte Tyme Tunes, 2001/Ji Branda Music Works, 2001/Minneapolis Guys Music, 2001
Performed by the Isley Brothers on the album *Eternal* (DreamWorks, 2001).

Lyricists & Composers Index

Aasim, Bambaataa Khayan *see*
  Bambaataa, Afrika
Adams, Bryan
  (Everything I Do) I Do It for You
  Inside Out
Adams, Ryan
  Answering Bell
  The Ballad of Carol Lynn
  Gonna Make You Love Me
  Jacksonville Skyline
  La Cienega Just Smiled
  New York, New York
Adams, William
  Request + Line
Adkins, James
  Bleed American
Adler, Lou
  Poor Side of Town
Adu, Helen *see* Sade
Afanasieff, Walter
  Broken Vow
  My Baby You
Afroman
  Because I Got High
Afu-Ra
  Bigacts Littleacts
Ahmadzai, Mirwais *see* Mirwais
Al-Baseer, Holly
  Cross the Border
Albarn, Damon
  Clint Eastwood
  Re-Hash

Alexakis, Arthur
  Rock Star
Alexander, Gregg
  I Can't Deny It
Alexander, Phalon
  Area Codes
Allamby, Darrell
  Crazy
Allen, Douglas, III
  Bizounce
Allen, John
  Oklahoma
Anders, Adam
  More Than That
Anderson, Keith
  Beer Run (B Double E Double Are
    You In?)
Anderson, Sunshine
  Heard It All Before
Angelettie, Deric
  I Just Wanna Love U (Give It 2 Me)
Anthony, Marc
  Celos
  My Baby You
April, John
  Fade
  It's Been Awhile
Arena, Tina
  Burn
Arie, India
  Video

Lyricists & Composers Index

Lyricists & Composers Index

Etheridge, Melissa
  I Want to Be in Love
Evans, Corey
  Take It to Da House
Evans, David *see* The Edge
Evans, Faith
  You Gets No Love
Evans, Sara
  Born to Fly
Evans, Sian
  Hide U
Eve
  Let Me Blow Ya Mind
  Who's That Girl
Fabian, Lara
  Broken Vow
Fabolous
  Can't Deny It
  Superwoman Pt. II
Fagenson, Anthony
  Here's to the Night
Fatboy Slim
  Weapon of Choice
Fehn, Christopher
  Left Behind
Ferreira, Hugo
  Breakdown
Fisher, Jamel
  Bad Boy for Life
Fitzpatrick, Colleen *see* Vitamin C
Flanagan, Michael
  In California
Flannery, Michael *see* One Track Mike
Flansburgh, John
  Boss of Me
Fleming, Charles
  Girls, Girls, Girls
Flowers, Michael *see* City, Mike
Fluckey, Tim
  Giving In
Folds, Ben
  Rockin' the Suburbs
Ford, Willa
  I Wanna Be Bad
Foreman, Joseph *see* Afroman
Foster, Radney
  I'm In

Frampton, Tijuan
  Can't Believe
Frank, David
  He Loves U Not
  This Is Me
Franklin, Georgette
  Love Don't Cost a Thing
Fraser, Maxwell
  We Come 1
Fratantuno, Michael, III
  Request + Line
Frazier, Charles
  Answer the Phone
  When It's Over
Frederiksen, Martin
  Fly Away From Here
  Jaded
Freeman, Rodger
  Papa's Got a Brand New Pigbag
The Fresh Prince
  Parents Just Don't Understand
Friend, Cliff
  Lovesick Blues
Furtado, Nelly
  I'm Like a Bird
  Turn Off the Light
Fusari, Robert
  Bootylicious
Gaines, Chan
  Baby If You're Ready
Gamble, Kenneth
  I Cry
Garfield, Wayne
  All for You
Garland, Hank
  Sugarfoot Rag
Garrett, Stephen
  Change the Game
  Rock the Boat
  We Need a Resolution
Garvin, Harold
  There It Is
Gass, Kyle
  Tribute
Gavin, John
  All Night Long
Gaye, Marvin
  Music

Lyricists & Composers Index

Lyricists & Composers Index

Jones, Teren
  Clint Eastwood
Jonsson, Gustav
  Bouncing off the Ceiling (Upside Down)
Jordan, Etterlene
  Ride Wit Me
Jordison, Nathan
  Left Behind
Judd, Cledus T.
  My Cellmate Thinks I'm Sexy
Juvenile
  Project Chick
  Set It Off
K-Ci
  Crazy
Kahan, Doug
  On a Night Like This
Kahne, David
  When It's Over
Kambon, Camara
  Family Affair
Kamen, Michael
  (Everything I Do) I Do It for You
Kanal, Tony
  Hey Baby
Karges, Matthew
  Answer the Phone
  When It's Over
Karlsson, Christian
  AM to PM
  Get It Up (The Feeling)
Katunich, Alex *see* Lance, Dirk
Kay, Jason
  Little L
Keating, Theo
  Start the Commotion
Keenan, Maynard
  Schism
Keith, Michael
  Dance With Me
  It's Over Now
  Peaches & Cream
Keith, Toby
  I'm Just Talkin' About Tonight
  You Shouldn't Kiss Me Like This
Keller, John
  Get Over Yourself

Kelley, Tim
  Missing You
Kelly, R.
  Contagious
  Feelin' on Yo Booty
  Fiesta
  The World's Greatest
Kennedy, Shelby
  I'm a Survivor
Kent, David
  Austin
Keys, Alicia
  Fallin'
Kid Rock
  Cocky
  Forever
  Picture
Kierulf, Brian
  I Wanna Be Bad
  That's How I Beat Shaq
Kilmore, Christopher *see* Kilmore, DJ
Kilmore, DJ
  Wish You Were Here
Kimbrough, Junior
  Done Got Old
King, Kerry
  Disciple
Kipner, Stephen
  He Loves U Not
  This Is Me
Kirchen, William
  Poultry in Motion
Kirkpatrick, Wayne
  Wrapped Up in You
Kirst, Alex
  V.I.P.
Kirst, Whitey
  V.I.P.
Knight, Christopher
  She Couldn't Change Me
Knighton, Willie
  Gasoline Dreams
Knobloch, James
  If My Heart Had Wings
Knowles, Beyonce
  Bootylicious
  Survivor

120

Lyricists & Composers Index

Lyricists & Composers Index

Pawlicki, Tommy
  Bouncing off the Ceiling (Upside
    Down)
Payne, Nora
  You Rock My World
Payne, Reginald
  Girls, Girls, Girls
Peake, Ryan
  How You Remind Me
  Too Bad
Pedersen, Johnny
  Lovin' You
Perren, Frederick
  Izzo (H.O.V.A.)
  My Baby
Perry, Linda
  Get the Party Started
Peters, Gretchen
  Inside Out
Peters, Juan
  Bizounce
Petey Pablo
  Raise Up
Pfrimmer, Don
  My Love Goes On and On
Philips, David
  In California
Phillip, Aaron see Afu-Ra
Picciotto, Guy
  Argument
Pierce, Christian
  Bodies
Pierson, Corey
  Uhhnnhh
Pineda, Allan
  Request + Line
Pizzonia, Shaun
  It Wasn't Me
Pomeranz, David
  One Minute Man
Poole, Barry see Judd, Cledus T.
Pop, Iggy
  V.I.P.
Porter, Denaun
  Fight Music
  Purple Pills
  Shit on You

Porter, Lamont
  Oochie Wally
Potts, Travon
  Mamacita
Power, Michael
  Leave It Up to Me
Price, Rodney
  Hey Baby
Prince
  Rainbow Children
  U Make My Sun Shine
Pritchard, Mike see Dirnt, Mike
Proby, Kimberley
  Baby If You're Ready
Quintana, Liza
  Out of Nowhere
Rademaker, Brent
  Yer Selfish Ways
Raekwon
  Never Be the Same Again
Ramirez, Twiggy
  Blood Pollution
Ramistella, John see Rivers, Johnny
Ransom, Mike
  Giving In
Ratcliffe, Simon
  Romeo
Rawlings, David
  Elvis Presley Blues
Redman
  Dog in Heat
  Part II
Redmon, Howard
  Who the Hell Are You?
Relf, Robert
  Girls, Girls, Girls
Reswick, Pam
  Burn
Rich, Denise
  Livin' for Love
Richards, Deke
  Izzo (H.O.V.A.)
  My Baby
Richie, Lionel
  Angel
Ritchie, Robert see Kid Rock
Rivers, Johnny
  Poor Side of Town

Lyricists & Composers Index

Lyricists & Composers Index

Important Performances Index

Songs are listed under the works in which they were introduced or given significant renditions. The index is organized into major sections by performance medium: Album, Movie, Musical, Performer, Revue, Television Show.

Album

141

Movie

Performer

Afu-Ra
Bigacts Littleacts
Aguilera, Christina
Lady Marmalade
Nobody Wants to Be Lonely
Air
How Does It Make You Feel
Alabama
When It All Goes South
Alien Ant Farm
Smooth Criminal
Alison Krauss & Union Station
Choctaw Hayride
The Lucky One
Allan, Gary
Right Where I Need to Be
Allen, Harley
I Am a Man of Constant Sorrow
In the Jailhouse Now
Allman Brothers Band
High Falls
Allure
Enjoy Yourself
American Hi-Fi
Flavor of the Weak
Amos, Tori
Strange Little Girl
Anderson, Sunshine
Heard It All Before
Andrews, Jessica
Who I Am
Anthony, Marc
Celos
My Baby You
Arie, India
Peaceful World
Video
Armstrong, Billie Joe
Unforgiven
Asleep at the Wheel
Ain't Nobody Here but Us Chickens
Sugarfoot Rag
A*Teens
Bouncing off the Ceiling (Upside
Down)
Avant
My First Love

Azul Azul
La Bomba
Babyface
There She Goes
Backstreet Boys
Drowning
More Than That
Shape of My Heart
Bad Seed
Uhhnnhh
Badu, Erykah
Didn't Cha Know
Sweet Baby
Ball, David
Riding With Private Malone
Barenaked Ladies
Falling for the First Time
Thanks That Was Fun
Basement Jaxx
Romeo
Bass, Lance
On the Line
BBMak
Ghost of You and Me
Beachwood Sparks
Yer Selfish Ways
Beanie Sigel
Change the Game
Beck
Diamond Dogs
Beck, Jeff
Dirty Mind
Bee Gees
This Is Where I Came In
Bennett, Tony
New York State of Mind
Bern, Dan
Turning Over
Beta Band
Squares
Better Than Ezra
Extra Ordinary
Bilal
Fast Lane
Soul Sista
Biz Markie
Girls, Girls, Girls

Television Show

Awards Index

A list of songs nominated for Academy Awards by the Academy of Motion Picture Arts and Sciences and Grammy Awards from the National Academy of Recording Arts and Sciences. Asterisks indicate the winners; multiple listings indicate multiple nominations.

2001

Academy Award
If I Didn't Have You*
May It Be
There You'll Be
Until
Vanilla Sky
Grammy Award
Ain't Nobody Here but Us Chickens
Ain't Nothing 'Bout You
Alive
All for You*
Always With Me, Always With You
Angel
Area Codes
Bad Boy for Life
Because I Got High
Beer Run (B Double E Double Are You In?)
Boss of Me*
Bring on the Rain
By Your Side
Can't Believe
Change the Game
Choctaw Hayride
Chop Suey!
Clint Eastwood
Cold, Cold Heart
Contagious

Crawling*
Didn't Cha Know
Didn't Leave Nobody but the Baby
Dig In*
Dirty Mind*
Disciple
Don't Let Me Be Lonely Tonight*
Don't Tell Me
Drops of Jupiter (Tell Me)
Drops of Jupiter (Tell Me)*
Elevation
Elevation*
Essence
Fallin'
Fallin'*
Family Affair
Fill Me In
Fly Away From Here
Foggy Mountain Breakdown*
Get Right With God*
Get Ur Freak On
Get Ur Freak On*
Gone
Grown Men Don't Cry
High Falls
Hit 'Em Up Style (Oops!)
Honest With Me
I Am a Man of Constant Sorrow*

I Dreamed About Mama Last Night
I Feel Loved
I Want Love
I Want to Be in Love
I Would've Loved You Anyway
I'm Already There
I'm Like a Bird
I'm Like a Bird*
Imitation of Life
Inside Out
It Wasn't Me
Izzo (H.O.V.A.)
Jaded
Lady Marmalade*
Left Behind
Let Me Blow Ya Mind*
Lifetime
Livin' It Up
Long Gone Lonesome Blues
A Long Walk
Love
A Love Before Time
Love of My Life
Lovesick Blues
The Lucky One*
Marie
Missing You
Ms. Jackson
Ms. Jackson*
Munster Rag
My Funny Friend and Me
My Kind of Girl
New York, New York
New York State of Mind
Nobody Wants to Be Lonely
O Death*
One Minute Man
One More Day
One More Time
Out of Nowhere
Peaceful World
Peaches & Cream
Planets of the Universe
Poultry in Motion

Put It on Me
Rain
Renegades of Funk
Reptile*
Ride Wit Me
Rock the Boat
Room 335
San Antonio Girl
Schism*
Shape of My Heart
Shine*
Short Circuit
Smooth Criminal
Someone to Call My Lover
The Space Between
Still
Strange Little Girl
Stuck in a Moment You Can't Get Out
  Of
Stuck in a Moment You Can't Get Out
  Of*
Sugarfoot Rag
Superman (It's Not Easy)
Superman Inside
Survivor*
There Is No Arizona
There You'll Be
This Is Love
U Remind Me*
Vampires
Video
W
Walk On
Walk On*
Weapon of Choice*
What Would You Do
When I Think About Angels
Where the Party At
Whispering a Prayer
Who We Be
Win
The Wizard
Yellow
You Rock My World
Your Disease

List of Publishers

A directory of publishers of the songs included in *Popular Music,* 2001. Publishers that are members of the American Society of Composers, Authors, and Publishers or whose catalogs are available under ASCAP license are indicated by the designation (ASCAP). Publishers that have granted performing rights to Broadcast Music, Inc., are designated by the notation (BMI). Publishers whose catalogs are represented by The Society of Composers, Authors and Music Publishers of Canada, are indicated by the designation (SOCAN). Publishers whose catalogs are represented by SESAC, Inc., are indicated by the designation (SESAC).

The addresses were gleaned from a variety of sources, including ASCAP, BMI, SOCAN, SESAC, and *Billboard* magazine. As in any volatile industry, many of the addresses may become outdated quickly. In the interim between the book's completion and its subsequent publication, some publishers may have been consolidated into others or changed hands. This is a fact of life long endured by the music business and its constituents. The data collected here, and throughout the book, are as accurate as such circumstances allow.

A

Acuff Rose Music (BMI)
65 Music Square West
Nashville, Tennessee 37203-3207

Adult Music (BMI)
c/o Carlos, Nielson, Peterson & Zan
630 S. Whitney Way, #150
Madison, Wisconsin 53711

Aerostation Corp. (ASCAP)
see Universal-MCA Music Publishing

Ain't Nothing but Funkin' (ASCAP)
see Warner-Chappell Music

Air Chrysalis Scandinavia
see Chrysalis Music

Air Control Music (ASCAP)
see EMI Music Publishing

J. Albert & Son Music (ASCAP)
c/o Carlin America, Inc.
126 East 38th St.
New York, New York 10016

Alexra Music (BMI)
c/o Voco Music
8360 Melrose Ave., 2nd Floor
Los Angeles, California 90069

List of Publishers

Ali-Aja Music (ASCAP)
   see Warner-Chappell Music

All Seeing Eye (ASCAP)
   see Universal-MCA Music Publishing

Almo/Irving
   1358 N. LaBrea
   Los Angeles, California 90028

Almo/Irving Music (BMI)
   1358 N La Brea
   Los Angeles, California 90028

Almo Music Corp. (ASCAP)
   2440 Sepulveda Blvd.
   Suite 1119
   Los Angeles, California 90064

Alpha Music
   Address Unavailable

Al's Street Music (ASCAP)
   see Warner-Chappell Music

Always Thinkin (ASCAP)
   160 E. Tamarack Ave.
   Inglewood, California 90301

Angel Music Ltd.
   Address Unavailable

Angel Notes Music (ASCAP)
   5076 Crooked Stick Way
   Las Vegas, Nevada 89113

Deric Angelettie Music (BMI)
   see EMI Music Publishing

Annotation Music (ASCAP)
   see Warner-Chappell Music

Anwa Music (ASCAP)
   see Almo Music Corp.

Appletree Songs
   Address Unavailable

April Blue Music (ASCAP)
   see EMI Music Publishing

APRS Music (BMI)
   see Peermusic

Arapesh Communications (ASCAP)
   c/o Spirit Two Music, Inc.
   137 Fifth Ave., 8th Flr.
   New York, New York 10010

Aruss Music
   Address Unavailable

Asiahtown Ent. (BMI)
   100 36 207th St.
   Queens Village, New York 11429

Avant Garde Music Publishing (ASCAP)
   c/o Margo Matthews
   5750 Wilshire Blvd., Suite 565W
   Los Angeles, California 90036

Axis Media Publishing (ASCAP)
   2860 Van Allen Blvd., Apt. 301
   Cleveland, Ohio 44120

B

Babyboys Little Pub Co (SESAC)
   see Warner-Chappell Music

Bambaataa Music (BMI)
   c/o Taylor
   3410 Dereimer Avenue, No. 4 M
   Bronx, New York 10475-1536

Barland Music (BMI)
   see Bug Music

Brandon Barnes Music (BMI)
   see Universal-MCA Music Publishing

Greg Barnhill Music (ASCAP)
   see Warner-Chappell Music

Baughnsongs (ASCAP)
   5814 Brentwood Trace
   Brentwood, Tennessee 37027

Teron Beal Songs (ASCAP)
   see BMG Songs Inc.

Beat Wise Music (BMI)
   see Warner-Chappell Music

Beechwood Music (BMI)
   see EMI Music Publishing

Beef Puppet Music (ASCAP)
see Universal-MCA Music Publishing

Belmont Mall Publishing (ASCAP)
see Sony ATV Tunes LLC

Better Half Music Co. (ASCAP)
c/o Estate of Jacqueline Hilliard
Howard E. Guedalia, Executor
David's Way
Bedford Hills, New York 10507

Forrest Richard Betts Music (BMI)
5125 Manattee Ave. West
Bradenton, Florida 33529

Beyonce Publishing (ASCAP)
c/o Music World Entertainment
9898 Bissonnete, Suite 625
Houston, Texas 77036

Bicameral Songs (BMI)
c/o Road Canon Music
10414 S W 238th St.
Vashon Island, Washington 98070-7656

Bicycle Music (ASCAP)
8075 W. 3rd St., Suite 400
Los Angeles, California 90048-4319

Bidnis Inc. (BMI)
c/o Stuart Ditsky CPA
733 Third Ave., 19th Floor
New York, New York 10017

Big Bizkit Music (ASCAP)
see Zomba Enterprises

Big Horse Music (BMI)
Address Unavailable

Big Mystique Music (BMI)
c/o Haber Corp.
16830 Ventura Blvd., Suite 501
Encino, California 91436

Big P Music (BMI)
c/o Richard Joseph
12300 Wilshire Blvd., No. 300
Los Angeles, California 90026

Big Yellow Dog Music (BMI)
c/o V.P. Publishing Administration
8 Music Square West
Nashville, Tennessee 37203

Bill-Lee Music (BMI)
c/o Williams Nichols
233 W. 99th St., Apt. 5E
New York, New York 10025-5016

Black Blessed Girl Music (ASCAP)
25590 Prospect Ave., Apt. 9C
Loma Linda, California 92354

Black Bull Music (ASCAP)
Attn: Stevland Morris
4616 Magnolia Blvd.
Burbank, California 91505

Black Ed Music (ASCAP)
41-06 10th St., #4E
Queens, New York 11101

Black Fountain Music (ASCAP)
see EMI Music Publishing

Black Hispanic Music (BMI)
see BMG Songs Inc.

Black Ice Publishing (BMI)
c/o Lisa Thomas Music Services
22287 Mulholland Hwy., #417
Calabasa, California 91302

Blakemore Avenue Music (ASCAP)
2004 Wedgewood Avenue
Nashville, Tennessee 37212

Blanc E Music (BMI)
c/o Burt Goldstein
156 W. 56th St., Ste. 1803
New York, New York 10019

Bleedy Eyes Music (ASCAP)
c/o Jason Green
728 San Bruno
Fresno, California 93710

Mary J. Blige Music (ASCAP)
see Universal-MCA Music Publishing

List of Publishers

Blondie Rockwell Music (ASCAP)
see Universal-MCA Music Publishing

Bloodheavy Music (BMI)
c/o Sendyk, Leonard & Co.
532 Colorado Ave.
Santa Monica, California 90401

Blotter Music (ASCAP)
see Windswept Pacific Entertainment

Blue Lamp Music (ASCAP)
see EMI Music Publishing

Blue's Baby Music (ASCAP)
see Universal-MCA Music Publishing

Blunts Guns and Funds (ASCAP)
see Famous Music Corp.

BMG Music (ASCAP)
1540 Broadway
New York, New York 10036

BMG Music Publishing Canada
Address Unavailable

BMG Songs Inc. (ASCAP)
8750 Wilshire Blvd.
Beverly Hills, California 90211

BNC Songs (ASCAP)
see Almo/Irving Music

Rob Bourdon Music (BMI)
see Zomba Songs

The Bourne Co. (ASCAP)
5 W. 37th St., 6th Floor
New York, New York 10018

Bovina Music (ASCAP)
see EMI Music Publishing

Boyletown Music (ASCAP)
Address Unavailable

Brea and Nea Music (BMI)
6635 Myrtle Ave.
Long Beach, California 90805

Breezeville Music Publishing (ASCAP)
c/o Songs of Peer Ltd.
5358 Melrose Ave., Suite 400
Los Angeles, California 90039

Breka Music (BMI)
PO Box 870275
New Orleans, Louisiana 70187-0275

Bridgeport Music (BMI)
c/o Jane Peterer Music
P.O. Box 526
Burlington, Vermont 05402-0526

Bristeasy Music (BMI)
c/o Roc Management
23 Old Quarry Rd.
Englewood, New Jersey 07631

Bro N' Sis Music (BMI)
c/o Carlin America, Inc.
126 East 38th St.
New York, New York 10016

Brandon Brody Music (BMI)
see Warner-Chappell Music

Bubba Gee Music (BMI)
see Warner-Chappell Music

Bucket Songs (ASCAP)
see BMG Songs Inc.

Buffalo Prairie Songs (BMI)
c/o V.P. Publishing Administration
8 Music Square West
Nashville, Tennessee 37203

Bug Music (BMI)
Bug Music Group
6777 Hollywood Blvd., 9th Fl.
Hollywood, California 90028-4601

Built on Rock Music (ASCAP)
c/o ICG Alliance Music
PO Box 24149
Nashville, Tennessee 37202

Henry Burnett Music (BMI)
see Bug Music

Butter Jinx Music (BMI)
c/o Margo Matthews
P.O. Box 92004
Los Angeles, California 90009-2004

Butterman Land Publishing (BMI)
see Universal-MCA Music Publishing

Buttflap Music (ASCAP)
c/o Kaplan Corp.
9454 Wilshire Blvd., #711
Beverly Hills, California 90212

C

C Sills Publishing (BMI)
see Music of Windswept

Caitlin Breanne Music (BMI)
see Bug Music

Cal IV Entertainment Inc. (ASCAP)
c/o Daniel Hill
808 19th Ave. South
Nashville, Tennessee 37203

Careers-BMG Music (BMI)
8750 Wilshire Blvd.
Beverly Hills, California 90211

Carmit Music (ASCAP)
see Len Freedman Music

Carpa Noche (ASCAP)
875 Morrison Ave., #8h
Bronx, New York 10473

Castrie Music (BMI)
3563 Bailey Rd.
Franklin, Tennessee 37064-9526

Champion Music Ltd.
Address Unavailable

Chargo Music (ASCAP)
see Bug Music

Chase Chad Music (ASCAP)
see EMI Music Publishing

Marky Chavez Publishing (BMI)
see EMI Music Publishing

Checkerman Music (BMI)
Address Unavailable

Cherry Lane Music (ASCAP)
6 E. 32nd St., 11th Fl.
New York, New York 10016

Cherry River Music (BMI)
6 East 32nd St., 11th Floor
New York, New York 10016

Cherryworks Music (BMI)
see Warner-Chappell Music

Chesterchaz Publishing (BMI)
see Zomba Songs

Chi-Boy Music (BMI)
c/o Gudvi, Chapnick & Company
15260 Ventura Blvd., Suite 2100
Sherman Oaks, California 91403

Children of the Forest Music (BMI)
c/o Manatt et al.
11355 W. Olympic Blvd.
Los Angeles, California 90064

Chocolate Factory Music (ASCAP)
Address Unavailable

Christ & Co. (BMI)
see Bug Music

Chrysalis Music (ASCAP)
Attn: Jeff Brabec
8500 Melrose, 2nd Floor
Los Angeles, California 90069

Chrysalis Songs (BMI)
see Chrysalis Music

Chuch Wagon Gourmet Music (ASCAP)
see Famous Music Corp.

Chunky Style Music (ASCAP)
see Disney Music Publishing

Chyna Baby Music (BMI)
see EMI Music Publishing

Clanger Songs (BMI)
8525 Santa Monica Blvd.
West Hollywood, California 90069

List of Publishers

Cloud 29 Publishing (ASCAP)
see Warner-Chappell Music

Coburn Music (BMI)
33 Music Square West
Suite 110
Nashville, Tennessee 37203

Colden Grey Ltd. (ASCAP)
c/o Red Light Management
PO Box 1911
Charlottesville, Virginia 22903

Cole-Arama Music (BMI)
10960 Wilshire Blvd., Suite 930
Los Angeles, California 90024-3712

Colgems-EMI Music (ASCAP)
see EMI Music Publishing

Colorscapes Publishing (BMI)
3412 Menlo Drive
Baltimore, Maryland 21215-3828

Comart Music (BMI)
3167 Beltagh Ave.
Wantagh, New York 11793

Janice Combs Music (BMI)
see EMI Music Publishing

Justin Combs Publishing (ASCAP)
see EMI Music Publishing

Common Green Music (BMI)
c/o Glieberman, Weise, and Associat
1600 Ventura Blvd., Suite 212
Encino, California 91436

Connotation Music (BMI)
see Warner-Chappell Music

Controversy Music (ASCAP)
c/o Ziffren Brittenham & Branca
2121 Ave. of the Stars
Los Angeles, California 90067

Don Cook Music (BMI)
c/o V.P. Publishing Administration
8 Music Square West
Nashville, Tennessee 37203

Copyright Control (ASCAP)
see Bug Music

Copyright Management Services (BMI)
1625 Broadway, 4th Floor
Nashville, Tennessee 37203

Copyright Net Music (BMI)
c/o V.P. Client Services
1625 Broadway, 4th Flr.
Nashville, Tennessee 37203

Coral Rock Music Corp.
see EMP Co.

Cotillion Music Inc. (BMI)
see Warner-Chappell Music

Country Road Music (ASCAP)
c/o Gelfand, Rennert & Feldman
1880 Century Park East
Los Angeles, California 90067

Cracklin' Music (BMI)
see Bug Music

Cross Keys Publishing (ASCAP)
attn: Donna Hilley
PO Box 1273
Nashville, Tennessee 37202

C2 It Music Publishing
Address Unavailable

Curb Congregation Songs (SESAC)
see Curb Songs

Curb Songs (ASCAP)
47 Music Square East
Nashville, Tennessee 37203-4324

Cyphercleff Music Publishing (ASCAP)
see EMI Music Publishing

Cyptron Music (BMI)
see EMI Music Publishing

D

D Style Music (ASCAP)
850 N. Ford St.
Burbank, California 91505

Da Bess Publishing
Address Unavailable

Da 12 Music (ASCAP)
see EMI Music Publishing

Dakoda House Music (ASCAP)
1217 Cedar Mill Square
Chesapeake, Virginia 23320

Dango Music (ASCAP)
c/o John T. Smith
10915 White Oak Ave.
Granada Hills, California 91344

Dannasongs (BMI)
see Famous Music Corp.

Dayspring Music (BMI)
3319 West End Ave., Suite 200
Nashville, Tennessee 37203-1074

Ddevil Music (ASCAP)
see Sony ATV Tunes LLC

De Roo Toons Music (ASCAP)
see EMI Music Publishing

Dead Game Publishing (ASCAP)
see Ruff Ryders Entertainment

Deadarm Music (ASCAP)
see Almo Music Corp.

Dee Mac Music (ASCAP)
8950 W. Olympic Blvd., #99
Beverly Hills, California 90211

Demis Hot Songs (ASCAP)
see EMI Music Publishing

Demon of Screamin Music (ASCAP)
see EMI Music Publishing

Denonation Music (SESAC)
see Warner-Chappell Music

Deondre's Bird (ASCAP)
see EMI Music Publishing

Derty Werks (ASCAP)
see EMI Music Publishing

Desert Storm Music (BMI)
Address Unavailable

Desmundo Music (ASCAP)
c/o Desmobile Productions, Inc.
4045 Sheridan Ave., Suite 256
Miami Beach, Florida 33140

Deston Songs (ASCAP)
see Sony ATV Tunes LLC

Diamond Rob Music (ASCAP)
see EMI Music Publishing

Donna Dijon Music (BMI)
see Universal-MCA Music Publishing

Dirty Dre Music (ASCAP)
see Universal-MCA Music Publishing

Disciples of Judra (ASCAP)
see BMG Songs Inc.

Disney Music Publishing (ASCAP)
500 S. Buena Vista St., MC 6174
Burbank, California 91521

Divine Mill Music (ASCAP)
see Warner-Chappell Music

Divine Pimp Music (ASCAP)
see BMG Songs Inc.

DJ Irv Publishing (BMI)
see Famous Music Corp.

Dole's Mix Music (BMI)
1025 Hillyer Ave.
Macon, Georgia 31204-3904

Dors-D Music (ASCAP)
54 Boerum St., #16E
Brooklyn, New York 11206

Dream Image IDG Publishing (BMI)
156 W. 56th St., 4th Fl.
New York, New York 10019

Dreamworks Songs (ASCAP)
see Cherry Lane Music

D2 Pro Publishing (ASCAP)
see Universal-MCA Music Publishing

Ducas Music (ASCAP)
see Universal-MCA Music Publishing

Dugong Songs (ASCAP)
see BMG Songs Inc.

Dungeon Rat Music (ASCAP)
see EMI Music Publishing

Duro Music (BMI)
see EMI Music Publishing

Dynacom Publishing (BMI)
c/o Sounds of Saints Studios
1812 Eider Ct.
St. Louis, Missouri 63133

Dynatone Publishing (BMI)
see Warner-Chappell Music

E

E Ballad Music (ASCAP)
see Warner-Chappell Music

E Beats Music (ASCAP)
see Warner-Chappell Music

E Equals Music (BMI)
see Warner-Chappell Music

E Two Music (ASCAP)
see EMI Music Publishing

EC Music Ltd.
Address Unavailable

Ecaf Music (BMI)
c/o V.P. Publishing Administration
8 Music Square West
Nashvillea, Tennessee 37203

Editorial Avenue (BMI)
Address Unavailable

Egotrippin Music (BMI)
Address Unavailable

Eight Inches Plus Publishing (BMI)
see Warner-Chappell Music

Eight Mile Style Music (BMI)
c/o Jeffrey Irwin Bass
1525 East Nine Mile Rd.
Ferndale, Michigan 48220

Eighty Six Sixty Music (BMI)
4434 Cornell St.
Dearborn Heights, Michigan 48125

El Cubano Music (BMI)
1901 Avenue of the Stars, 11th Flr.
Los Angeles, California 90067

Ella and Gene's Son's Music (ASCAP)
see EMI Music Publishing

Elvis Mambo Music (ASCAP)
see Music of Windswept

Emelia Music (SESAC)
c/o 360 Music
360 N. La Cienega Blvd.
Los Angeles, California 90048-1925

EMI-April Music (ASCAP)
see EMI Music Publishing

EMI-Blackwood Music Inc. (BMI)
see EMI Music Publishing

EMI-Full Keel Music (ASCAP)
see EMI Music Publishing

EMI Longitude Music (BMI)
see EMI Music Publishing

EMI Mills Music (ASCAP)
see EMI Music Publishing

EMI Music Publishing
810 Seventh Ave.
New York, New York 10019

EMI Music Publishing Italia (BMI)
Address Unavailable

EMI Music Publishing Ltd.
Address Unavailable

EMI Sosaha Music (BMI)
see EMI Music Publishing

EMI Unart Catalogue (BMI)
see EMI Music Publishing

EMI United Partnership Ltd.
Address Unavailable

EMI-Virgin Music (ASCAP)
see EMI Music Publishing

EMI-Virgin Songs (BMI)
see EMI Music Publishing

EMP Co. (BMI)
The Entertainment Co.
40 W. 57th St.
New York, New York 10019

Empire International Music (BMI)
see EMI Music Publishing

Ensign Music (BMI)
see Famous Music Corp.

EPHCY Publishing (ASCAP)
see Universal-MCA Music Publishing

Escatawpa Songs (BMI)
c/o Frascogna Courntey PLLC
P.O. Box 23126
Jackson, Mississippi 39225-3126

Essex Music International (ASCAP)
c/o The Richmond Organization
11 West 19th St.
New York, New York 10011

Estes Park Music (BMI)
2803 Bransford Ave.
Nashville, Tennessee 37204-3101

Evergleam Music (BMI)
c/o Glieberman, Weise & Associates
1600 Ventura Blvd., Suite 212
Encino, California 91436

Ez Elpee Music (BMI)
c/o Lamont J. Porter
825 Boyton Ave., Apt. 5B
Bronx, New York 10473

F

Faith Force (ASCAP)
see Zomba Enterprises

Fake and Jaded Music (BMI)
c/o Manatt et al.
11355 W. Olympic Blvd.
Los Angeles, California 90064

Famous Music Corp. (ASCAP)
10635 Santa Monica Blvd.
Ste. 300
Los Angeles, California 90025

Fatima & Bara Outlet (ASCAP)
526 4th St.
Darby, Pennsylvania 19023

Fifty Four Vill Music (BMI)
Address Unavailable

Fingaz Goal Music (ASCAP)
see EMI Music Publishing

First Avenue Music Ltd.
Address Unavailable

First and Gold Publishing (BMI)
see Warner-Chappell Music

Five for Fighting Music (BMI)
see EMI Music Publishing

563 Music Publishing (ASCAP)
see Zomba Enterprises

Five Superstars (ASCAP)
see Almo Music Corp.

5700 Park Music (BMI)
see EMI Music Publishing

Floyd's Dream Music (BMI)
4409 Park Ave.
Nashville, Tennessee 37209-3652

Flybridge Tunes (BMI)
see EMI Music Publishing

Flyte Tyme Tunes (ASCAP)
see EMI Music Publishing

List of Publishers

For Chase Muzic (ASCAP)
  see Windswept Pacific Entertainment

Foray Music (SESAC)
  see EMI Music Publishing

Forces Beyond Productions
  Address Unavailable

Foreign Imported Productions (BMI)
  555 Jefferson Ave.
  Miami, Florida 33139

Four Forty Magnum Music (BMI)
  101 Saddlebow Rd.
  Bell Canyon, California 91307

4T4 Music (SESAC)
  see Windswept Pacific Entertainment

Fox Film Music Corp. (BMI)
  PO Box 900, Bldg. 18
  Beverly Hills, California 90213

Foxy Dead Girl Music (ASCAP)
  see EMI Music Publishing

Free From the Man Songs
  Address Unavailable

Len Freedman Music
  1482 E. Valley Rd., #400
  Santa Barbara, California 93108

From the Pit Publishing
  Address Unavailable

Dwight Frye Music (BMI)
  72 Madison Ave., 8th Floor
  New York, New York 10016

Fugazi Songs (BMI)
  c/o Lunar Atrocities Ltd.
  2706 N. 4th St.
  Arlington, Virginia 22201-1606

Fun with Goats Music (ASCAP)
  see EMI Music Publishing

Funky Noble Productions (ASCAP)
  see Famous Music Corp.

Future Furniture (ASCAP)
  see EMI Music Publishing

G

G Chills Music (BMI)
  see Cherry River Music

G Matt Music (ASCAP)
  see Warner-Chappell Music

Gabburr Tunes (ASCAP)
  see Universal-MCA Music Publishing

Gaje Music (BMI)
  Address Unavailable

Gan Zmira (ASCAP)
  see Famous Music Corp.

Garianno Music Publishing (SESAC)
  see Music on the Net

Gibb Brothers Music (BMI)
  see BMG Music

Gimme Some Hot Sauce Music (ASCAP)
  see Famous Music Corp.

Gizzo Music (BMI)
  1908 Alsace Lane
  Marietta, Georgia 30008

Glasco Music, Co. (ASCAP)
  PO Box 8470
  Universal City, California 91608

Global Jukebox Publishing (BMI)
  c/o Bedlock, Levine & Hoffman
  99 Park Ave., Suite 1600
  New York, New York 10016

Gloria's Boy Music (ASCAP)
  see EMI Music Publishing

Gnat Booty Music (ASCAP)
  see Chrysalis Music

God's Child Music (ASCAP)
  c/o 4 Track Records
  415 19th St., #A
  Huntington Beach, California 92648

Gold and Iron Music Publishing (ASCAP)
see Warner-Chappell Music

Golddaddy Music (ASCAP)
see EMI Music Publishing

Good High Music (ASCAP)
450 Hickory Glen Lane
Atlanta, Georgia 30311

Goodie Mob Music (BMI)
see Chrysalis Music

Gotta Groove Music (ASCAP)
see EMI Music Publishing

Gottahaveable Music (BMI)
see Windswept Pacific Entertainment

GQ Romeo Music (BMI)
see Warner-Chappell Music

Grave Lack of Talent Music (BMI)
c/o Provident Financial Management
10345 W. Olympic Blvd., 2nd Floor
Los Angeles, California 90064

Gravitron Music (SESAC)
PO Box 120904
Nashville, Tennessee 37212-0904

Green Daze Music (ASCAP)
1100 Third St.
San Rafael, California 94901

Greenfund (ASCAP)
see Warner-Chappell Music

Greenhorse Music (BMI)
PO Box 186
Waring, Texas 78074

Grey Ink Music (ASCAP)
1608 N. Cahuenga Blvd., #203
Hollywood, California 90028

Griff Griff Music (ASCAP)
see EMI Music Publishing

Grosse Point Harlem Publishing (BMI)
Address Unavailable

Ground Control Music (BMI)
see EMI Music Publishing

H

Hale Yeah Music (SESAC)
see EMI Music Publishing

Haleem Music (ASCAP)
c/o PNSW
156 West 56th St., 4th Floor
New York, New York 10019

Mark Hammond Music (ASCAP)
c/o ICG Alliance Music
PO Box 24149
Nashville, Tennessee 37202

Hand Picked Songs (ASCAP)
4011 Wayland Drive
Nashville, Tennessee 37215

Happy Hemp Music (ASCAP)
see Universal-MCA Music Publishing

Happy Mel Boopy's Cocktail Lounge (BMI)
see Zomba Songs

Hapsack Music (BMI)
see Copyright Management Services

Hard Working Black Folks (ASCAP)
see Warner-Chappell Music

O J Harper Publishing (ASCAP)
1355 Velvet Creek Glen
Marietta, Georgia 30060

Sammy Harpo Music (BMI)
Address Unavailable

Harrindur Publishing (BMI)
see Famous Music Corp.

Hatley Creek Music (BMI)
see EMI Music Publishing

Havana Brown Publishing (BMI)
see Songs of Universal

Scott Hendricks Corporation (ASCAP)
see Warner-Chappell Music

Hennesy for Everyone (BMI)
15250 Ventura Blvd., Ste. 900
Sherman Oaks, California 91403-3221

Herbilicious Music (ASCAP)
see EMI Music Publishing

High Priest Publishing (BMI)
see Famous Music Corp.

Hitco South (ASCAP)
see Windswept Pacific Entertainment

Hollis Music, Inc.
c/o The Richmond Organization
11 W. 19th St.
New York, New York 10011-4209

Hollohart Music (ASCAP)
Address Unavailable

Hood Classic (ASCAP)
c/o Roynet Music
224 West 30th St., Suite 1007
New York, New York 10001

Hot Heat Music (ASCAP)
see EMI Music Publishing

House of Bram (ASCAP)
3877 Couchville Pike
Hermitage, Tennessee 37076

Howdy Skies Music (ASCAP)
3629 Robin Road
Nashville, Tennessee 37204

Hunglikeyora (ASCAP)
see EMI Music Publishing

Mark Hybner Publishing (ASCAP)
1600 17th Ave. South
Nashville, Tennessee 37212

Hydroponic Music (BMI)
946 N. Croft Ave.
Los Angeles, California 90069-4204

I

I Want My Daddy's Records (ASCAP)
see Warner-Chappell Music

Icepickjay Publishing (ASCAP)
40 West 135th St., #3F
New York, New York 10037

Idiotic Biz (ASCAP)
see EMI Music Publishing

Enrique Iglesias Music (ASCAP)
see EMI Music Publishing

Ill Will Music (ASCAP)
see Zomba Enterprises

I'm Nobody Music (ASCAP)
see Warner-Chappell Music

I'm With the Band Music (ASCAP)
see Warner-Chappell Music

In Tha Blood Music (ASCAP)
1706 East 174th St.
Bronx, New York 10472

Incomplete Music (BMI)
1841 Broadway
New York, New York 10023

Indolent Sloth Music (ASCAP)
see Warner-Chappell Music

Instinct Music (ASCAP)
207 Oak Drive
Franklin, Tennessee 37064

Irving Music Inc. (BMI)
2440 Sepulveda Blvd., Suite 119
Los Angeles, California 90064

J

J Brasco (ASCAP)
322 Bainbridge Street, #7C
Brooklyn, New York 11233

J Music for Stixx and Tones (ASCAP)
9648 Olive, #388
St. Louis, Missouri 63132

J-Rated Music (ASCAP)
see EMI Music Publishing

Jack Walroth Music (ASCAP)
1818 15th St., #5
San Francisco, California 94103

Jackie Frost Music
Address Unavailable

Jagged Music
Address Unavailable

Mick Jagger Music
Address Unavailable

Jahque Joints (SESAC)
see Universal-MCA Music Publishing

Tommy Lee James Songs (BMI)
see Still Working for the Man Music

Jat Cat Music Publishing (ASCAP)
see Universal-MCA Music Publishing

Jay Bird Alley Music (BMI)
500 Bishop St., Suite A5
Atlanta, Georgia 30318

Jay E's Basement (ASCAP)
see Universal-MCA Music Publishing

Jazzmen Publishing (ASCAP)
52 Spier Dr.
South Orange, New Jersey 07079

Jazzy Jeff & Fresh Prince (ASCAP)
see Zomba Enterprises

Jeepney Music Publishing (BMI)
13701 Riverside Dr., 8th Flr.
Sherman Oaks, California 91423

Jelinda Music (BMI)
c/o Barry De Vorzon
1323 E. Valley Rd.
Montecito, California 93108

Jerk Awake Music (ASCAP)
c/o Manatt Phelps & Phillips
11355 W. Olympic Blvd.
Los Angeles, California 90064

Rodney Jerkins Productions (BMI)
see EMI Music Publishing

Fred Jerkins Publishing (BMI)
see Famous Music Corp.

Jersey Girl Music (ASCAP)
see EMI Music Publishing

Ji Branda Music Works (ASCAP)
see EMI Music Publishing

Jim Rooster Music (ASCAP)
2502 Eagle St.
Houston, Texas 77004

Jimmie Fun Music
Address Unavailable

Jobete Music Co. (ASCAP)
see EMI Music Publishing

Joelsongs (BMI)
1880 Century Park East, Suite 1600
Los Angeles, California 90067

Jogar Music Publishing
Address Unavailable

Tim Johnson Music Publishing (BMI)
4159 Fairview Rd.
Columbia, Tennessee 38401-1357

Jonathan Three Music (BMI)
see Lastrada Music

Jones Music America (ASCAP)
c/o RZO
110 West 57th St., 7th Floor
New York, New York 10019

Lucy Jones Music (BMI)
see Warner-Chappell Music

Hudson Jordan Music (ASCAP)
see Almo Music Corp.

Jose Luis Gotcha Music (BMI)
c/o Penalty Records
902 Broadway
New York, New York 10010

Josh Nick Music (ASCAP)
see Zomba Songs

June Bug Alley (ASCAP)
  see Sony ATV Tunes LLC

K

Kababa Music (ASCAP)
  c/o Pen Music Group
  1608 N. Palmas Ave., Suite 1024
  Los Angeles, California 90028

Kalinmia Music (ASCAP)
  945 East Paces Ferry Rd.
  Suite 2610
  Atlanta, Georgia 30326

Keepin It Real How Bout You Music (BMI)
  see Warner-Chappell Music

R. Kelly Publishing (BMI)
  see Zomba Songs

Kierulf Songs (BMI)
  see Zomba Songs

Killa Cam Music (ASCAP)
  1339 Queen Anne Rd.
  Teaneck, New Jersey 07666

King Swing Music (BMI)
  see EMI Music Publishing

Stephen A. Kipner Music (ASCAP)
  see EMI Music Publishing

Kirsti Mannasongs (ASCAP)
  c/o Bradley Music Mgmt., Inc.
  1100 18th Ave. South
  Nashville, Tennessee 37212

Kling Kling Music (ASCAP)
  see Windswept Pacific Entertainment

Klown County (ASCAP)
  see EMI Music Publishing

J. Fred Knobloch Music (ASCAP)
  7128 Birch Bark Drive
  Nashville, Tennessee 37221

Kenji Kobayashi Music (BMI)
  see Zomba Songs

Kohlslaw Music (BMI)
  see Warner-Chappell Music

Kumbaya (ASCAP)
  see Zomba Enterprises

L

Lady Ashley Music (BMI)
  c/o Fine, Weinberger and Co.
  156 West 56th St.
  New York, New York 10019

Larga Vista Music (ASCAP)
  c/o BPJ Administration
  PO Box 218061
  Nashville, Tennessee 37221

Las Chivas Music (BMI)
  Address Unavailable

Lastrada Music (ASCAP)
  1344 Broadway, Suite 208
  Hewlett, New York 11557

LBN Publishing (ASCAP)
  see EMI Music Publishing

LBR Music (ASCAP)
  c/o Provident Financial Management
  10345 W. Olympic Blvd., 2nd Floor
  Los Angeles, California 90064

Lehsem Music LLC (ASCAP)
  c/o U.S. Music & Media
  8756 Holloway Drive
  Los Angeles, California 90069

Lehsem Songs (BMI)
  8756 Holloway Drive
  Los Angeles, California 90069

Lerocious Music (BMI)
  see Bug Music

Less Than Zero Music (BMI)
  c/o Manatt et al.
  11355 W. Olympic Blvd.
  Los Angeles, California 90064

LG Wells Music (BMI)
Address Unavailable

Life Force Music (BMI)
c/o The Royalty Network
224 West 30th St., Suite 1007
New York, New York 10001

Lil Lu Lu Publishing (BMI)
see EMI Music Publishing

Lil' Nettie Music
Address Unavailable

Lil Strat Songs (SESAC)
116 Choctaw Dr.
Hendersonville, Tennessee 37075-4642

Line One Publishing (ASCAP)
see EMI Music Publishing

Liquid Liquid Publishing (BMI)
45 Carmine St., No. 3B
New York, New York 10014

Lit Up Music (ASCAP)
see Famous Music Corp.

Lithium Glass Music (ASCAP)
see EMI Music Publishing

Little Chatterbox Music (BMI)
1025 16th Ave. South, Suite 202
Nashville, Tennessee 37212

Little Dume Music (ASCAP)
see Disney Music Publishing

Little Idiot Music (BMI)
see Warner-Chappell Music

Little Macho Music (ASCAP)
Address Unavailable

Little Mike Music (BMI)
Address Unavailable

Little Miss Music (ASCAP)
see EMI Music Publishing

Live Slow Music (BMI)
4159 Arno Rd.
Franklin, Tennessee 37064

Livingsting Music (ASCAP)
see Warner-Chappell Music

Billy Livsey Music (BMI)
5745 Knob Road
Hillwood Place
Nashville, Tennessee 37209

LMNO Pop Music (ASCAP)
see EMI Music Publishing

Lonte Music (ASCAP)
122 Sisson St.
Howardville, Missouri 63869

Loud Mouse Music (BMI)
see EMI Music Publishing

Love Ranch Music (ASCAP)
see EMI Music Publishing

Luchi Publishing (BMI)
PO Box 070412
Brooklyn, New York 11207

Ludacris Music Publishing (ASCAP)
see EMI Music Publishing

M

M L E Music (ASCAP)
c/o W. F. Leopold Management
4425 Riverside Drive, Suite 102
Burbank, California 91505

M W E Publishing (ASCAP)
9898 Bissonnet, Suite 625
Houston, Texas 77036

Maanami Music (ASCAP)
see EMI Music Publishing

Magic Man Music
Address Unavailable

Maine Money (ASCAP)
526 S. 4th St.
Darby, Pennsylvania 19023

Major Bob Music (ASCAP)
1111 17th Ave. South
Nashville, Tennessee 37212

List of Publishers

Marsky Music (BMI)
  Address Unavailable

Marty Bags Music (ASCAP)
  see Chrysalis Music

Mascan Music (ASCAP)
  see Warner-Chappell Music

Mashamug Music (BMI)
  PO Box 44298
  CinCinnati, Ohio 45244-0298

Mass Confusion Productions (ASCAP)
  see Warner-Chappell Music

Maverick Music (ASCAP)
  see Warner-Chappell Music

Maximus Nashville (ASCAP)
  c/o Maximus Entertainment Group
  1303 16th Ave. South
  Nashville, Tennessee 37212

MCA Music Publishing (ASCAP)
  see Universal-MCA Music Publishing

Davel McKenzie Publishing (ASCAP)
  1174 Hillock Crossings
  Virginia Beach, Virginia 23455

Mcmore Music (BMI)
  c/o Copyright Net Music
  1625 Broadway, 4th Floor
  Nashville, Tennessee 37203

Mcud Music (ASCAP)
  see Zomba Enterprises

Swifty McVay Publishing (ASCAP)
  18511 Santa Rosa
  Detroit, Michigan 48221

Me Again Music (BMI)
  Address Unavailable

Means Family Publishing (ASCAP)
  11301 W. Olympic Blvd., #306
  Los Angeles, California 90064

Medina Sounds Music (BMI)
  see EMI Music Publishing

Meeengya Music (ASCAP)
  see Universal-MCA Music Publishing

Mel Boopie Music (BMI)
  c/o Chapman, Bird & Grey
  1990 South Bundy Drive, Suite 200
  Los Angeles, California 90025

Memphisto Music (ASCAP)
  see Universal-MCA Music Publishing

Mewtwo Music (ASCAP)
  see Cherry Lane Music

Mick Hits Music (ASCAP)
  c/o Michael Wayne Hiter
  PO Box 110375
  Nashville, Tennessee 37222

Mighty Nice Music (BMI)
  c/o Bluewater Music Corp.
  PO Box 120904
  Nashville, Tennessee 37212

Mijac Music (BMI)
  see Warner-Chappell Music

Mijohkel
  Address Unavailable

Mika Magic Music (BMI)
  Address Unavailable

Mike City Music (BMI)
  see Warner-Chappell Music

Mike Curb Music (BMI)
  c/o Brad Kennard
  47 Music Square East
  Nashville, Tennessee 37203

Milene Music (ASCAP)
  c/o Opryland Music Group
  P.O. Box 128469
  Nashville, Tennessee 37212

Milk Chocolate Factory (ASCAP)
  see Sony ATV Tunes LLC

Milksongs (ASCAP)
  see Warner-Chappell Music

Minneapolis Guys Music (ASCAP)
  see EMI Music Publishing

Miracle Creek Music (ASCAP)
  c/o Morgan Creek Music Group
  4000 Warner Blvd., Bldg. 76
  Burbank, California 91522

Miss Bessie Music (ASCAP)
  c/o Provident Financial Mgmt.
  10345 Olympic Blvd.
  Los Angeles, California 90064

Miss Hazel Music (BMI)
  17060 Central Pike
  Lebanon, Tennessee 37090

Mistral Entertainment Music (ASCAP)
  Address Unavailable

Mo-Down Muzik (ASCAP)
  see EMI Music Publishing

Mo Loving Music (ASCAP)
  2646 Streamview Drive
  Odenton, Maryland 21113

Molosser Music (ASCAP)
  c/o Provident Financial Management
  10345 W. Olympic Blvd.
  Los Angeles, California 90064

Money Mack Music (BMI)
  100 James Drive, Suite 130
  St. Rose, Louisiana 70087

Charlie Monk Music (ASCAP)
  3001 Hobbs Rd.
  Nashville, Tennessee 37215

Monkids Music (SESAC)
  PO Box 150768
  Nashville, Tennessee 37215-0768

Monowise Ltd.
  Address Unavailable

Montalupis Music (BMI)
  c/o Glieberman, Weise & Associates
  1600 Ventura Blvd., Suite 212
  Encino, California 91436

MPL Communications (ASCAP)
  41 West 54th St.
  New York, New York 10019

Mr. Manatti Music (BMI)
  see EMI Music Publishing

Mtume Music (BMI)
  217 Mayhew Drive
  South Orange, New Jersey 07079-1310

Mugsy Boy Publishing (BMI)
  c/o Joshua Michael Schwartz
  14 Tuscany Drive
  Jackson, New Jersey 08527

Murlyn Songs
  Address Unavailable

Murrah Music (BMI)
  1109 16th Ave. South
  PO Box 121623
  Nashville, Tennessee 37212-2304

Music Alley (ASCAP)
  c/o ICG Alliance Music
  PO Box 24149
  Nashville, Tennessee 37202

Music on the Net (SESAC)
  c/o Copyright Management Int.
  1625 Broadway, 4th Floor
  Nashville, Tennessee 37203-3138

Music Pieces (BMI)
  740 N. La Brea Ave., 2nd Floor
  Los Angeles, California 90038

Music River Publishing (BMI)
  Memphis State University
  Memphis, Tennessee 38152-0001

Music Sales Corp. (ASCAP)
  257 Park Ave. S., 20th Fl.
  New York, New York 10010

Music That Music (ASCAP)
  see EMI Music Publishing

Music in Three (BMI)
  Address Unavailable

Music of Windswept (ASCAP)
    see Windswept Pacific Entertainment

Muszewell Music (ASCAP)
    see Sony ATV Music

My Blue Car Music (ASCAP)
    see Warner-Chappell Music

My Own Chit Publishing (BMI)
    see EMI Music Publishing

Mycenae Music Publishing Co. (ASCAP)
    Martin Cohen
    740 N. LaBrea Ave.
    Los Angeles, California 90038

N

Nakita's Publishing (ASCAP)
    see Cherry Lane Music

Nate Dogg Music (BMI)
    see Sony ATV Music

Nay D Publishing (ASCAP)
    3287 N. Tamarind Ave.
    Rialto, California 92377

Nelstar Publishing (SOCAN)
    Address Unavailable

Neon Mule Music Publishing (ASCAP)
    see Warner-Chappell Music

New Don Songs (ASCAP)
    c/o FBMM, Inc.
    PO Box 331549
    Nashville, Tennessee 37203

New Enterprises Music (BMI)
    see Fox Film Music Corp.

New Hayes Music (ASCAP)
    c/o FBMM, Inc.
    PO Box 331549
    Nashville, Tennessee 37203

Roger Nichols Music Inc.
    Address Unavailable

98 Degrees and Rising (ASCAP)
    see EMI Music Publishing

Nivrac Tyke Music (ASCAP)
    see EMI Music Publishing

Noise Dog Productions (BMI)
    8500 Melrose Ave., #207
    West Hollywood, California 90069

Kenny Nolan Publishing (ASCAP)
    c/o Peter C. Bennett
    503 N. Elm Dr.
    Beverly Hills, California 90210

Nolivian Songs (BMI)
    see Bug Music

Nondisclosure Agreement Music (BMI)
    see Zomba Songs

Noontime South (SESAC)
    see Warner-Chappell Music

Notable Music Co. (ASCAP)
    see Warner-Chappell Music

Notorious Kim Music (BMI)
    c/o Queen Bee Entertainment
    23 Old Quarry Rd.
    Englewood, New Jersey 07631

Nueva Ventura Music (ASCAP)
    c/o Ventura Music Group
    13644 S W 142nd Ave., Suite D
    Miami, Florida 33186

Nuyorican Publishing (BMI)
    see Sony ATV Tunes LLC

Nyrraw Music (ASCAP)
    see EMI Music Publishing

O

Obanyon Music (BMI)
    c/o Integrated Copyright
    PO Box 24149
    Nashville, Tennessee 37202

Obo Itself
    Address Unavailable

Odar Publishing (ASCAP)
see Warner-Chappell Music

Oglirifica (ASCAP)
see Warner-Chappell Music

Old Crow Music (BMI)
see Warner-Chappell Music

Olos Eoj Publishing (ASCAP)
see Famous Music Corp.

On My Mind Music (ASCAP)
see Universal-MCA Music Publishing

Ooky Spinalton Music (ASCAP)
see EMI Music Publishing

Organized Noize Music (BMI)
see Windswept Pacific Entertainment

O'Shaughnessy Ave Music (ASCAP)
273 Glenstone Circle
Brentwood, Tennessee 37027

Our Write Music (BMI)
320 Marshall St.
Bellwood, Illinois 60104

P

Pacific Wind Music (SESAC)
see Windswept Pacific Entertainment

Pal-Dog Music (ASCAP)
see Music Sales Corp.

Pang Toon Music (ASCAP)
see EMI Music Publishing

Panola Park Music (ASCAP)
see Warner-Chappell Music

Pare Publishing (SOCAN)
Address Unavailable

Parker Music (BMI)
c/o Fantasy, Inc.
2600 Tenth St.
Berkeley, California 94710

Parnassus Productions (ASCAP)
see Sony ATV Tunes LLC

Pearl White Music (BMI)
see EMI Music Publishing

Peermusic (BMI)
810 7th Ave.
New York, New York 10019-5818

Peermusic III LTD (BMI)
5358 Melrose Blvd.
Suite 400
Los Angeles, California 90038

Pener Pig Publishing (BMI)
see Universal-MCA Music Publishing

Pennemunde Music (ASCAP)
c/o Provident Financial Management
10345 W. Olympic Blvd.
Los Angeles, California 90064

Peppermint Stripe Music (BMI)
1203 Ferdinand
Detroit, Michigan 48209

Perfect Songs Ltd.
Address Unavailable

Pimp Yug (ASCAP)
see Warner-Chappell Music

Pinkys Playhouse (ASCAP)
4469 Ventura Canyon Ave., Apt. E205
Sherman Oaks, California 91423

Elsie Louise Pitts Music (BMI)
see Universal-MCA Music Publishing

Pixar Talking Pictures (ASCAP)
c/o Robert Taylor
1011 W. Cutting Blvd.
Richmond, California 94804

Pladis Music (ASCAP)
see EMI Music Publishing

Plant Publishing II (SOCAN)
Address Unavailable

Platinum Firm Music (ASCAP)
see Zomba Enterprises

List of Publishers

Platinum Plow (ASCAP)
see Warner-Chappell Music

Platinum World Publishing (BMI)
see Soundtron Tunes

Plaything Music (ASCAP)
c/o Cohen and Cohen
740 North Brea Ave., 2nd Floor
Los Angeles, California 90038

Plum Tree Tunes
Address Unavailable

Plumbshaft Ltd.
Address Unavailable

Plus 1 Publishing (ASCAP)
4901 Vineland Rd., Suite 340
Orlando, Florida 32811

Pocket Change Publishing
Address Unavailable

Porch Pickin' Publishing (ASCAP)
1044 Beech Tree Lane
Brentwood, Tennessee 37027

Portable Music Company (BMI)
see Warner-Chappell Music

Pounding Drool (ASCAP)
see Renfield Music Publishing

Proceed Music (BMI)
c/o The Royalty Network
224 West 30th St., Suite 1007
New York, New York 10001

Protoons Inc. (ASCAP)
77 Chambers St., 4th Floor
New York, New York 10073

Pubco Music (BMI)
c/o Rykomusic
101 Charles Drive, Bldg. 1
Bryn Mawr, Pennsylvania 19010

Purple Crayon Music (ASCAP)
see Sony ATV Music

Q

Q Zik Music (BMI)
740 N. La Brea Ave., 1st Floor
Los Angeles, California 90038

R

Rap Tracks Publishing (ASCAP)
see Warner-Chappell Music

Reach Global Songs (BMI)
see Reach Music International

Reach Music International (ASCAP)
217 E. 86th St., Ste. 117
New York, New York 10028

Real Diamonds (ASCAP)
see Zomba Enterprises

Realsongs (ASCAP)
Attn: Diane Warren
6363 Sunset Blvd., Ste. 810
Hollywood, California 90028

Renfield Music Publishing (ASCAP)
72 Madison Ave., 8th Floor
New York, New York 10016

Reswick Songs (ASCAP)
see EMI Music Publishing

Revolvair Sarl (BMI)
Address Unavailable

Rhett Rhyme Music (ASCAP)
see BMG Songs Inc.

Rick's Music Inc. (BMI)
see Warner-Chappell Music

Right Bank Music (ASCAP)
22761 Pacific Coast Hwy., Suite 227
Malibu, California 90265

Rightsong Music (BMI)
see Warner-Chappell Music

Rio Bravo Music (BMI)
1111 17th Ave. South
Nashville, Tennessee 37212-2203

Roastitoasti Music (ASCAP)
see Wixen Music

Sharon Robinson Songs (ASCAP)
see Wixen Music

Bruce Robison Music (BMI)
c/o Bluewater Music Corp.
PO Box 120904
Nashville, Tennessee 37212-0904

Rock the Mike Music (BMI)
see EMI Music Publishing

Golly Rogers Music (BMI)
see EMI Music Publishing

Rokstone Music
Address Unavailable

Romeo Cowboy Music (ASCAP)
see EMI Music Publishing

Rope & String Music (ASCAP)
120 Williamson Court
Murfreesboro, Tennessee 37128

Route Six Music (BMI)
7531 Pewitt Rd.
Franklin, Tennessee 37064-9272

Rude Gal Music (ASCAP)
c/o Madolyn Wind Ludlum
201 Oakland Ave., #3
Oakland, California 94611

Ruff Ryders Entertainment (ASCAP)
312 West 53rd St., Suite 208
New York, New York 10019

Runyon Ave (ASCAP)
see EMI Music Publishing

Rye Songs (BMI)
c/o V.P. Publishing Administration
8 Music Square West
Nashville, Tennessee 37203

Rykomusic (ASCAP)
101 Charles Drive, Bldg. #1
Bryn Mawr, Pennsylvania 19010

S

Sailor Music (ASCAP)
PO Box 12680
Bellevue, Washington 98111

St. Julien Music (ASCAP)
see Universal-MCA Music Publishing

Salaam Remi Music (ASCAP)
see EMI Music Publishing

Sand B Music (BMI)
1528 Rising Glen Rd.
Los Angeles, California 90069-1226

Satcher Songs (ASCAP)
see Sony ATV Tunes LLC

Michael Angelo Saulsberry Music (ASCAP)
16601 Ventura Blvd., Suite 506
Enano, California 91436

Say Uncle Music (BMI)
5100 Nevada Ave.
Nashville, Tennessee 37209-3333

Scarlet Moon Music (BMI)
Address Unavailable

Scarlet Rain Music (ASCAP)
PO Box 2362
Richmond, California 94802

Screen Gems-EMI Music Inc. (BMI)
see EMI Music Publishing

Screenchoice Ltd.
Address Unavailable

Sea Gayle Music (ASCAP)
see EMI Music Publishing

Sell the Cow Music (BMI)
see Warner-Chappell Music

Erick Sermon Enterprises (ASCAP)
see Zomba Enterprises

Seven Peaks Music (ASCAP)
see Disney Music Publishing

List of Publishers

Shack Suga Entertainment (ASCAP)
9648 Olive, #388
St. Louis, Missouri 63132

Shae Shae Music (ASCAP)
see Wixen Music

Shakin Baker Music (BMI)
c/o Howard Comart, C.P.A.
1775 Broadway, Suite 532
New York, New York 10019-1903

Shakur al Din Music (ASCAP)
see Windswept Pacific Entertainment

Damon Sharpe Music (ASCAP)
see Warner-Chappell Music

Victoria Shaw Songs (SESAC)
see Sony ATV Tunes LLC

Shep and Shep Publishing (ASCAP)
see Almo Music Corp.

Show You How Daddy Ball Music (ASCAP)
see EMI Music Publishing

Silent Movies for the Blind
Address Unavailable

Silliwak (ASCAP)
see EMI Music Publishing

Silver Fiddle Music (ASCAP)
see Wixen Music

Silverback Music (ASCAP)
c/o Carlos Garcia
30-18 91st St., Suite 2F
East Elmhurst, New York 11369

Paul Simpson Music (BMI)
2181 Blossomwood Dr.
Oviedo, Florida 32765

Simranch Songs (ASCAP)
PO Box 1701
Mt. Juliet, Tennessee 37121

Six July Publishing (BMI)
see Famous Music Corp.

6 Mo Shots Music (BMI)
141-25 182nd St.
Queens, New York 11413

Six O One Broadway Music (BMI)
PO Box 370391
Key Largo, Florida 33037

Slavery Music (BMI)
194 10 E. 65 Crescent
Fresh Meadows, New York 11365

E. O. Smith Music (BMI)
see Wixen Music

Smooth As Silk Publishing (ASCAP)
740 N. La Brea Ave., 2nd Floor
Los Angeles, California 90038

Smooth C Publishing (BMI)
c/o Anita McCloud
7024 Louise Rd.
Philadelphia, Pennsylvania 19138

S'More Music (ASCAP)
see Universal-MCA Music Publishing

Sneaka Rican Music (ASCAP)
c/o Double Platinum Productions
199 Hackensack Plank Rd., 1st Fl.
Weehawken, New Jersey 07807

So Kol Productions (ASCAP)
3287 N. Tamarind Ave.
Rialto, California 92377

So So Def Music (ASCAP)
see EMI Music Publishing

Songs of Alexhan (ASCAP)
see Warner-Chappell Music

Songs of Lastrada (BMI)
see Lastrada Music

Songs of Peer (ASCAP)
5358 Melrose Ave., Suite 400
Los Angeles, California 90039

Songs of Teracel (BMI)
c/o V.P. Publishing Administration
8 Music Square West
Nashville, Tennessee 37203

Songs of Universal (BMI)
see Universal-MCA Music Publishing

Songs of Windswept Pacific (BMI)
see Windswept Pacific Entertainment

Sonic Grafitti (ASCAP)
see EMI Music Publishing

Sony/ATV Discos Music Publishing (ASCAP)
605 Lincoln Rd.
Miami Beach, Florida 33139

Sony ATV Music (ASCAP)
550 Madison Ave.
New York, New York 10022

Sony ATV Songs LLC (BMI)
8 Music Square West
Nashville, Tennessee 37203

Sony ATV Tunes LLC (ASCAP)
8 Music Square West
Nashville, Tennessee 37203

Sony Tunes (ASCAP)
see Sony ATV Music

Soul Child Music (ASCAP)
see Universal-MCA Music Publishing

Soulife Copyright Holdings (BMI)
Address Unavailable

Souljah Music (ASCAP)
see Famous Music Corp.

Sound Island Music
Address Unavailable

Soundtron Tunes (BMI)
c/o Butter Jinx Music
P.O. Box 92004
Los Angeles, California 90009

Southfield Road Music (BMI)
c/o Manatt et al.
11355 W. Olympic Blvd.
Los Angeles, California 90064

Special Rider Music (SESAC)
PO Box 860, Cooper Sta.
New York, New York 10276

Mark Alan Springer Music (BMI)
2967 McCanless Rd.
Nolensville, Tennessee 37135

Srand Music (BMI)
see Zomba Songs

Stalmach Music (BMI)
Address Unavailable

Stamen Music (BMI)
c/o Marsha, Haney, Gelfand et al.
333 Market St., 18th Floor
San Francisco, California 94105

Starks Publishing
Address Unavailable

Sticky Green (ASCAP)
c/o Brent Robinson
4724 S. Greenwood, #3W
Chicago, Illinois 60615

Still Working for the Man Music (BMI)
1625 Broadway
Nashville, Tennessee 37203

Stone Diamond Music (BMI)
see EMI Music Publishing

Stonebridge Music (ASCAP)
see Bicycle Music

Scott Storch Music (ASCAP)
see TVT Music

Strange Beautiful Music (ASCAP)
c/o Siegel, Feldstein & Doffin
2020 Union St.
San Francisco, California 94123

Stridgirl Music (ASCAP)
see BMG Songs Inc.

List of Publishers

The Strokes Band Music (ASCAP)
c/o Wiz Kid Management
123 East 7th St.
New York, New York 10021

Stuck in the Throat (ASCAP)
see Famous Music Corp.

Sugar Hill Music Publishing, Ltd.
96 West St.
Englewood, New Jersey 07631

Sugarfuzz Music (BMI)
P.O. Box 467399
Atlanta, Georgia 31146-7399

Superstar Maker Music (BMI)
8525 Santa Monica Blvd.
West Hollywood, California 90069

Suti Music (ASCAP)
see EMI Music Publishing

Sam Swap Publishing (ASCAP)
c/o Ali K. Jones
8851 Northcrest
St. Louis, Missouri 63147

Swear By It Music (ASCAP)
see Zomba Enterprises

Sweet Woo Music (SESAC)
see Warner-Chappell Music

Swette Ya' Music (ASCAP)
see Warner-Chappell Music

Sy Vy Music (ASCAP)
Box 2264
Hollywood, California 90078

T

T Girl Music LLC (BMI)
902 Broadway, 13th Floor
New York, New York 10010

Tabulous Music (ASCAP)
see Windswept Pacific Entertainment

Tairona Songs Ltd.
Address Unavailable

Talbot Music Publishing (BMI)
2 Music Circle South
Nashville, Tennessee 37203

Tallest Tree Music (ASCAP)
see Cherry Lane Music

Tamarama Music (ASCAP)
8610 West Knoll Dr.
Los Angeles, California 90069

Tannyboy Music (BMI)
11355 W. Olympic Blvd.
Los Angeles, California 90064-1614

Tayminster Ltd.
Address Unavailable

TCF Music Publishing (ASCAP)
see Twentieth Century-Fox Music Corp.

Teamsta Entertainment Music (BMI)
c/o The Royalty Network
224 West 30th St., Suite 1007
New York, New York 10001

Teflon Hitz (ASCAP)
c/o Sheldon Harris
11 Jackson Ave.
Scarsdale, New York 10583

Temporary Music (BMI)
see Warner-Chappell Music

Tennman Tunes (ASCAP)
see Zomba Enterprises

Tentative Music (BMI)
PO Box 15083
New Orleans, Louisiana 70175

Bob D Terry Publishing (BMI)
6946 Blue Holly Ct.
Forestville, Maryland 20747

Tessa Publishing (BMI)
c/o CMI
1625 Broadway, 4th Floor
Nashville, Tennessee 37203-3138

Thanks To Van Publishing (ASCAP)
74 North Cedar Lake Drive West
Columbia, Missouri 65203

Them Damn Twins Music (ASCAP)
see EMI Music Publishing

Thirty Two Mile Music (BMI)
see Warner-Chappell Music

Thom Tunes
Address Unavailable

Thousand Mile Inc. (BMI)
see Bug Music

Three EB Publishing (BMI)
c/o EGM, Inc.
1040 Mariposa, Suite 200
San Francisco, California 94107-2520

Cori Tiffani Publishing (BMI)
see Sony ATV Songs LLC

Tiltawhirl Music (BMI)
c/o Byrom and Associates
PO Box 128461
Nashville, Tennessee 37212

Time for Flytes Music (BMI)
1876 Independence Square
Dunwoody, Georgia 30338

Time For My Breakfast (ASCAP)
5044 Maytime Lane
Culver City, California 90230

TJ Beats Publishing (BMI)
Address Unavailable

Todski Music (BMI)
see Warner-Chappell Music

Tokeco Tunes (BMI)
1107 17th Ave. South
Nashville, Tennessee 37212

Toolshed Music (ASCAP)
see EMI Music Publishing

Touched by Jazz Music (ASCAP)
see EMI Music Publishing

Touchstone Pictures Music and Songs
(ASCAP)
see Disney Music Publishing

Toy Toy Music (ASCAP)
9648 Olive, #388
St. Louis, Missouri 63132

TP Songs (ASCAP)
4529 Ben Ave.
Studio City, California 91607

Travon Music (ASCAP)
see Universal-MCA Music Publishing

Tray Tray's Music (ASCAP)
c/o Tracey Davis
15665 Willow Dr.
Fontana, California 92337

Treat Baker Music (SOCAN)
c/o NGB Inc.
579 Richmond St. W., Ste. 401
Toronto, Ontario M5V1Y6
Canada

Tree Publishing (BMI)
c/o V.P. Publishing Administration
8 Music Square West
Nashville, Tennessee 37203

Tremonti Stapp Music (BMI)
72 Madison Ave., 8th Floor
New York, New York 10016

Trescadecaphobia Music (BMI)
c/o Troy Jamerson
110 33 157th St.
Jamaica, New York 11433

Tru Stylze Music (ASCAP)
see Famous Music Corp.

Trudysong Music (ASCAP)
c/o ICG Alliance Music
PO Box 24149
Nashville, Tennessee 37202

True North Music (ASCAP)
see Warner-Chappell Music

Ttuff Ttony Music (BMI)
PO Box 571
Asbury Park, New Jersey 07712

Tuff Huff Music (BMI)
see Zomba Songs

Tunes on the Verge of Insanity (ASCAP)
see Famous Music Corp.

Tuono Music (BMI)
1901 Avenue of the Stars
Los Angeles, California 90067

Turkey On Rye Music (ASCAP)
c/o Nick Ben-Meir, CPA
652 North Doheny Drive
Los Angeles, California 90069

TVT Music (ASCAP)
23 E. 4th St.
New York, New York 10003

Twang Thang Music (ASCAP)
2318 Maplecrest Dr.
Nashville, Tennessee 37214

Twentieth Century-Fox Music Corp. (ASCAP)
P.O. Box 900
Music Dept., Bldg. #18
Beverly Hills, California 90213

Twenty Nine Black Music (BMI)
96 West St.
Englewood, New Jersey 07631

Two Hundred Miles From Civilization (BMI)
c/o 11th Hour Entertainment Group
1800 Second St., Suite 712
Sarasota, Florida 34236

2855 Music (BMI)
500-425 Carrall St.
Vancouver, British Columbia V6B 6E3
Canada

2000 Watts Music (ASCAP)
see EMI Music Publishing

Two Twenty Nine Music (BMI)
see Wixen Music

Tycon Music (BMI)
Address Unavailable

Tziah Music (BMI)
see Warner-Chappell Music

U

Uh Oh Entertainment (ASCAP)
see EMI Music Publishing

Un Rivera Publishing (BMI)
see Untertainment Music

Uncle Bobby Music (BMI)
see EMI Music Publishing

Uncle Jake's Music (BMI)
304 Woodland Hills Rd.
White Plains, New York 10603

Undeas Music (BMI)
266 Washington Ave., Suite D16
Brooklyn, New York 11205

Underachiever Music (BMI)
c/o King, Purtich, Holmes et al.
1900 Avenue of the Stars, 25th Floo
Los Angeles, California 90067-4506

Unichappell Music Inc. (BMI)
see Warner-Chappell Music

Universal-MCA Music Publishing (ASCAP)
2440 Sepulveda Blvd., Suite 100
Los Angeles, California 90064-1712

Universal Musica (ASCAP)
420 Lincoln Rd., Suite 306
Miami Beach, Florida 33139

Universal Polygram International Pub.
(ASCAP)
see Universal-MCA Music Publishing

Universal-Polygram International Tunes
(SESAC)
99440 Collection Center Dr.
Chicago, Illinois 60693-0994

Universal Songs of Polygram Intntl. (BMI)
see Universal-MCA Music Publishing

Untertainment Music (ASCAP)
3 East 28th St., 9th Floor
New York, New York 10016

UR-IV Music (ASCAP)
see EMI Music Publishing

V

Valentine's Day Songs (BMI)
see Warner-Chappell Music

Townes Van Zandt Music (ASCAP)
4569 Poplar Wood Rd.
Smyrna, Tennessee 37167

Vaporeon Music (BMI)
see Cherry River Music

Phil Vassar Music (ASCAP)
see EMI Music Publishing

Velvet Apple Music (BMI)
1880 Century Park East, Suite 1600
Los Angeles, California 90067

Vibe Crusher Music (BMI)
see Almo/Irving

Vibzelect (BMI)
c/o V.P. Publishing Administration
8 Music Square West
Nashville, Tennessee 37203

Virginia Beach Music (ASCAP)
see Warner-Chappell Music

Vix Mix Music (BMI)
8726 24th Ave.
Brooklyn, New York 11214

W

W B M Music (SESAC)
see Warner-Chappell Music

Wajero Sound (BMI)
Address Unavailable

Wally World Music (ASCAP)
c/o Jonathan Wexler, CPA
5203 Desmond St.
Oakland, California 94618

Steve Wariner Music (BMI)
P.O. Box 157
Nolensville, Tennessee 37135

Warner-Barham Music LLC
Address Unavailable

Warner Brothers Music Ltd.
Address Unavailable

Warner-Chappell Music (ASCAP)
10585 Santa Monica Blvd.
Los Angeles, California 90025

Warner-Tamerlane Publishing (BMI)
see Warner-Chappell Music

Chris Waters Music (BMI)
c/o V.P. Publishing Administration
8 Music Square West
Nashville, Tennessee 37203

Waters of Nazareth Publishing (BMI)
see EMI Music Publishing

WB Music Publishing (ASCAP)
see Warner-Chappell Music

Webo Girl Publishing (ASCAP)
see Warner-Chappell Music

Wedgewood Avenue Music (BMI)
see Windswept Pacific Entertainment

Weitz House Publishing
Address Unavailable

Welsh Witch Music (BMI)
c/o V.P. Publishing Administration
8 Music Square West
Nashville, Tennessee 37203

Wenonga Music (BMI)
c/o V.P. Publishing Administration
8 Music Square West
Nashville, Tennessee 37203

List of Publishers

Stephen Werfel Songs (ASCAP)
see EMI Music Publishing

Whiskey Gap Music (BMI)
c/o Trio Productions
1026 15th Ave. South
Nashville, Tennessee 37212-2414

White Rhino Music (BMI)
c/o Stephen Finfer
23 East 4th St.
3rd Floor
New York, New York 10003-7023

Who Owns Your Music (ASCAP)
c/o Spur of the Moment Musik
3478 Columbia Drive
La Verne, California 91750

Whorga Music (ASCAP)
see EMI Music Publishing

Wide Ocean Music (BMI)
303 Charlesgate Place
Nashville, Tennessee 37215

Wiedwacker Music (ASCAP)
see Bug Music

Wil Coll Publishing (BMI)
8648 Olympic Blvd., Suite 103
Los Angeles, California 90035

Will I Am Music (BMI)
13701 Riverside Dr., 8th Floor
Sherman Oaks, California 91423

Willdawn Music (ASCAP)
1105 17th Ave. South
Nashville, Tennessee 37212

Kim Williams (ASCAP)
see Sony ATV Music

Wind Tiger Music (BMI)
Address Unavailable

Windover Lake Songs (ASCAP)
9696 Culver Blvd., Suite 203
Culver City, California 90232

Windswept Music
Address Unavailable

Windswept Pacific Entertainment (ASCAP)
9320 Wiltshire Blvd., Suite 200
Beverly Hills, California 90212-3217

Wirzma Publishing (BMI)
see Bug Music

Without Anna Music (ASCAP)
1700 Hayes St. Bldg.
Nashville, Tennessee 37203

Wixen Music (BMI)
24025 Park Sorrento, Suite 130
Calabasas, California 91302

Wonderland Music (BMI)
see Disney Music Publishing

Wood and I Music (BMI)
30 Music Square West
Nashville, Tennessee 37203

World of the Dolphin Music (ASCAP)
see Universal-MCA Music Publishing

Wretched Music (ASCAP)
see Warner-Chappell Music

Wu-Tang Publishing (BMI)
see BMG Music

Wunderwood Music (BMI)
see EMI Music Publishing

X

X Flat Minor Music (ASCAP)
c/o Aaron Sperske
1332 Sutherland St.
Los Angeles, California 90026

Y

Yab Yum Music (BMI)
c/o V.P. Publishing Administration
8 Music Square West
Nashville, Tennessee 37203

Yee Haw Music (ASCAP)
see Warner-Chappell Music

Yellow Man Music (BMI)
c/o Vernon Brown and Co.
10 Bank St., Suite 820
White Plains, New York 10606

Young Dude Publishing (ASCAP)
see Universal-MCA Music Publishing

Z

Zachary Creek Music (BMI)
c/o Morgan Creek Music Group
4000 Warner Blvd., Bldg. 76
Burbank, California 91522-0002

Zen of Iniquity (ASCAP)
see Almo Music Corp.

Zollia Publishing (BMI)
1225 Steiner, No. 511
San Francisco, California 94115

Zomba Enterprises (ASCAP)
138 West 25th St., 8th Floor
New York, New York 10001

Zomba Management Publ. Ltd.
Address Unavailable

Zomba Songs (BMI)
137-139 W. 25th St
New York, New York 10001

Zovektion Music (ASCAP)
see BMG Songs Inc.

ISBN 0-7876-3313-5